RARE MOMENTS

JEANETTE WILSON

Zenith Publishing

National Library of New Zealand Cataloguing-in-Publication Data

Wilson, Jeanette, 1962-
Rare moments / Jeanette Wilson.
ISBN 1-877365-12-2
1. Wilson, Jeanette, 1962- 2. Channeling (Spiritualism) I. Title.
133.91—dc22

Zenith Publishing
PO Box 752
49-55 Rimu Street extn
New Plymouth
New Zealand
www.zenithpublishing.co.nz

First published in 2005 by Zenith Publishing
Printed by Publishing Press Ltd
Cover photograph by Frances Oliver

To Alessandra's mum
& others like her who
lovingly guide & help
us from the spiritual
side of life

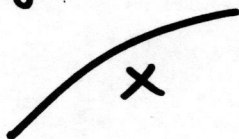

x

Contents

Foreword

How many of us have wondered about death at different times in our lives? I know I have, hearing of an unexpected passing, or of a tragedy on the news. Whenever I found myself thinking about such matters I would quickly bring my thoughts back to something more positive – why? Why didn't I want to think about dying? Why didn't I want to think about a loved one passing? Had I known then what I know now, would it have been any different? Yes, absolutely. Now, I know that there is no death. How do I know that? Because I talk to the spirits of 'deceased' people every day.

Do I fear death? No. Why? Because in 10 years I haven't come across a single spirit who wanted to be back here. Yes, some had painful transitions from this physical dimension into the next but often that helped them to separate from their physical form more easily. It also made it easier for their loved ones here to let them go, as they didn't want to continue to see them in pain and suffering.

I have learned much over the past 10 years, since seeing Spirit for the first time, and I continue to learn. I have been, and continue to be, a keen student for all life has to teach me.

Before spiritually awakening in 1994, I was completely sceptical of mediums and clairvoyants, mainly because I had not witnessed any demonstrations of genuine psychic ability. Now, I travel around the world, demonstrating to audiences that there is no death. Every show I do is different and I never know quite what to expect. I continue to learn, as no two messages are the same, no two audiences are the same and no two spirits are the same.

I ask my guides in the spiritual dimensions for twice as much laughter as tears, and they usually give it. For example when Mary came through from spirit world with a plastic washing-up bowl, her daughter laughed, "That was definitely Mum – she had a mild form of dementia and took her plastic washing-up bowl with her everywhere! She even washed herself in it!"

Our loved ones are so keen to let us know they are there, and that they are alright, that they will use whatever they can to let us know – playing with lights, phones, televisions, doorbells, calling our names and appearing to us in dreams. At the shows, it never ceases to amaze me the stories people tell about their loved ones. If we all talked about our experiences more, it would not only help us heal, but help us realise these experiences are not so rare – they are happening all the time to a great many people from all walks of life.

The number of children able to see Spirit also seems to be increasing – and their abilities need to be recognised rather than dismissed as imaginings or psychological problems. At some shows as many as 50% of the audience know of a child who is able to see or sense 'Spirit'.

There are so many questions that the people I come across want answers to: What happens when we die? Do we all go to the same place? What happens to people who commit suicide? What happens to children? Some I can answer and some I can't – I have to say I do not know. What I do know though is that the knowledge I now have has helped me enormously to live a more meaningful and more peaceful life, and the feedback I have had from others is that it has helped them too.

In this book then I share some of my favourite insights with you, together with stories from the shows, in the hope that it will do the same for you.

NOTE: The essence of the stories is factual. All took place either in the UK or New Zealand. However, for each of the stories, names and certain details have been deliberately changed to protect individuals' privacy.

For example, a communication with a brother may have been changed to a communication with a sister, all other details remaining the same.

A Secret Song

"I can't take my mum home like this." The speaker was a young dark-haired girl who was very close to tears and steadfast in her resolve. She looked me straight in the eye, "Mum has so looked forward to tonight. She pinned all her hopes on Dad coming through, and he hasn't. Please will you see her? I wouldn't normally ask but I feel I just have to." She looked down to her feet. She was clearly very upset and what touched me was that she was asking not for herself but for her mother. I also sensed her awkwardness at asking; she was not someone who would normally be so forthright.

I was tired after doing a two-hour mediumship show and making the four-hour trip to the venue. Mediumship to a large audience takes huge amounts of energy and concentration. I had already seen two other members of the audience privately because of the nature of their messages from loved ones in the spiritual dimensions. It was after 10pm, I had been on the road since lunchtime and I was really ready to switch off from listening to spirits and to have my head and body back.

I am always present in my body when doing mediumship and always 'in charge', but it is nevertheless good when it is over and I can go back to being more 'normal'. I quickly glanced around the room, which had been filled to capacity just half an hour before. It had been a wonderful evening full of inspiring stories and messages. There had been occasional tears but much laughter as spirits reminded their loved ones of the happy times together and the loving memories they had shared. It had been a good show. Now the room was empty apart from a lady who I quickly deduced must be this young girl's mother, and my partner Andrew, who was busy packing away our sound equipment.

Tired as I was, I felt the daughter's desperation and agreed to see her mum and found myself walking over to where she was sitting. I pulled up a chair and slipped off my show shoes, which although they looked fabulous, were extremely uncomfortable by this time of the evening. I explained to the young girl's mum that I couldn't promise that I could make a connection because my energy was low after the show; it had been a long day.

As I sat with the young girl and her mum on seats at the front of the empty room, the girl's mum eagerly passed me over a small colour photograph. As soon as I held it in my hand I heard the name Brian in my head and "Brian" came out of my mouth before I knew it. "Yes, his name was Brian," his wife immediately confirmed. I knew he had passed very quickly. Again these facts were confirmed as correct. Then Brian's spirit, which now felt to be inside of me and to my left, put all his energy and attention into my teeth. I knew he had not died from something wrong with his teeth. People just do not die from problems with their teeth. So what did he mean? I asked the lady if she had something wrong with her teeth. "Not to speak of," she said. "What do you mean?" I asked internally. I was puzzled. "Show me what you mean," I silently instructed Brian in my head. Still my teeth tingled. It didn't make sense.

The lady was pleased that I had been able to give her Brian's name but explained that long before her husband died they had agreed to let each other know there was an 'afterlife', if they found there was one, by singing a particular song. Could I tell her the song? My heart sank. I was tired. Part of me felt that surely giving her his name straight away should be enough proof, as Brian is not that common a name. Then I put myself in her shoes. There was a lot of love between her and her late husband and his passing was still very painful for her and her young daughter. Brian had given me his

3

name easily enough so maybe the song would come easily too. I asked internally to be told the name of the song. Again, my teeth started feeling funny. I insisted that instead of doing that, Brian concentrate on giving me the song, the one he and his wife had promised each other. "I don't understand the message about the teeth. Forget that," I said internally. "Please give me the name of the song."

Nothing My mind was an absolute blank. My mind often wasn't that blank during meditation. I was at a complete loss as to what it meant. Blankness. Silence. "Perhaps he was trying to give me *The Sound of Silence*, a song by Simon and Garfunkel," I thought. "Unlikely," I reasoned in my head, as it would have been easier and quicker to play me the tune, as it was familiar to me.

From my experience, loved ones in the spiritual dimensions often give me information through reminding me of something I already know or have had experience with. It is the easiest way for them to work with me. If, for example, they want to give me a particular name they may show me someone I know who has the same name. If they want to give me a particular feeling they will remind me of a time that I felt that way. Therefore, if I didn't know the song it would be very difficult for me to 'receive' it. Difficult, but not impossible, I reassured myself – in the past

I had talked successfully with people of different nationalities whose language I did not understand at all and still communication had been possible.

Logic told me that the chances of me knowing the song were very slim, as the lady was of a different generation to myself. However, despite my tiredness and the seeming impossibility of what I was being asked to do, something made me persist. A good five minutes must have passed. I sat with my eyes closed, completely silent. Finally, the lady asked if she should tell me. "No, I will give it another few minutes," I said. "Don't ever tell anyone the song, because if you do you will never know for sure. You'll never have your proof. I am tired but it is worth trying for a few minutes more." The lady's daughter was intrigued and moved closer to us; she had not known about the agreement and couldn't imagine which song her father and mother would have chosen.

I tried to relax once more. I felt myself fully in my body, feeling my fingers and my toes and noticing my breathing. It is important when listening to loved ones in the spiritual dimensions to be fully conscious and not to try too hard. I wished I was not so tired; I find it is much easier to bring through information when I am energised. As soon as I noticed that I was 'wishing', I immediately stopped myself, as that kind of energy works against the connections. I have to

5

be fully present with a clear, focused mind because I can't hear Spirit when my head is filled with my own thoughts. I again focused on being in my body and observing my breathing. I knew that I could not risk passing on the wrong song. It would be better to say nothing than to try and fail. Again I noticed that I was in my head, thinking and worrying about passing on the wrong song.

"Relax," I told myself. Once more I put all my energy and focus into feeling myself in my body and noticing my breathing, just observing it. Not changing it in any way, just observing it. This time I managed to stay relaxed and focused for more than a few seconds. After a few moments my teeth started tingling again and this time I saw a pink toothbrush and a blue toothbrush with smiling faces and dancing feet as well. I 'remembered' a childhood song my mother used to sing me, 'You're a pink toothbrush, I'm a blue toothbrush, have we met somewhere before? You're a pink toothbrush and I think toothbrush, that we met by the bathroom door . . .' I couldn't remember all the words. It had been years since I had heard the song but the tune was as clear as day in my head and so were the images.

My logical brain intervened. Surely that can't be it? Why on earth choose that song? It was hardly romantic. It wasn't my place to judge, I reasoned. It was the only song I had been given and I had been given it in words, music and images all at once. I still had the fear about singing the 'wrong' song, but now that I had the message in three ways, I was more confident so decided to sing the first few bars. "You're a pink toothbrush, I'm a blue toothbrush, have we met somewhere before?" I sang. For a split second the lady just stared at me and I wondered quite how she was going to react. Was I right or wrong? Then tears began spilling down the lady's face and then the daughter's. These were tears of joy! I knew I'd got the correct song. Of all the thousands of possible songs, I had sung the very one they had promised to sing to one another if there was an 'afterlife'. I had given her the exact proof she had wanted so desperately.

At moments such as this it is hard to put how I feel into words. Time stands still. It's as though all my experiences in this lifetime have brought me to a particular moment in time and every little thing that has happened to me has been significant; that there's some 'Divine Order' to this world in which we live. I feel I have the best job in the world, that I am truly blessed being able to do what I do. All that I have been through and continue to go through is worthwhile for moments like this. I had made the right decision choosing to leave my successful career as a bank manager, to explore the spiritual aspects of life and develop my own personal abilities.

I felt tears welling in my eyes. The daughter was amazed. She didn't even recognise the song and her mum had to explain why they had chosen it. They had had their discussion long before Brian's passing and chosen it because it was the most unlikely song someone would sing from the 'other side'; it was a song that no one would be able to guess. It was wonderful proof of his survival! Brian was as ecstatic about getting the message through to his loved ones, as his loved ones were about receiving it. His joyous feelings were filling my body along with the joy of his wife and daughter.

Suddenly I realised that Brian had been trying to give me the song from the start. His wife confirmed that she had realised that too, but didn't like to say anything as she didn't want to give me any clues. She wanted to know for sure. Brian had been trying to give me the song through my feeling sense by making my teeth tingle and I hadn't picked it up. I *was* tired! Brian had been determined to get his message through and used all three channels or senses: clairvoyance (clear seeing) – the images of the toothbrushes dancing; clairaudience (clear hearing) – the lyrics and music, and clairsentience (clear sensing) – the tingling teeth. His determination had paid off despite my tiredness. Both mother and daughter were extremely grateful for what had happened – and I was too. If I had not persevered, and I nearly hadn't, she would not have received her song and she would have gone away very disappointed. She would not have known for sure that her husband did live on, because the song they had promised to sing would not have been sung.

Sometimes the responsibility of what I do weighs heavily on my shoulders. In this case I was grateful for all the help I had received and I felt very humble that Brian was able to come through me in the way that he did. It isn't me who makes the loved ones come through, I don't will them through. They come through using their free will and on a frequency of love. I just have to stay relaxed and keep my mind and body clear, ready to 'receive' what they convey. I find feelings and concepts are easier to convey than precise words and I've found that the more practice I have the better I get. The trick seems to be not to try, but to relax and just allow the messages through, taking care not to over interpret what I see, hear or sense.

The communication with Brian finished. We exchanged hugs – his wife and I first of all and then the daughter and I. Brian in spirit wanted to hug them each once more. I felt him in my body as we hugged. People ask me how I see/sense spirit and each one is different. Some show me themselves as they were when they died and some show themselves in their prime. Some are in my head and some I see alongside the living person. Some I simply feel in my body, as I did with Brian. As I hugged them I felt his feelings towards both his wife and his daughter and tears filled my eyes again. He loved them both so much. Brian wasn't sad though, because he was with them all the time and he was closer to them than he had ever been before as now none of his emotional baggage from this lifetime got in the way. He was able to love them 'completely'.

The way it has been explained to me is that we come onto this earth plane as open, sensitive beings, capable of giving and receiving enormous levels of love. If you have ever held a baby in your arms and truly connected with it I am sure you will be able to relate to what I am saying.

As babies we are totally loving, totally open beings and all we have known of life is our warm soft experience of being within the womb floating in warm liquid with only dulled sounds and the ever-present heartbeat of our mother. All of a sudden something is pushing us out, out into a place of bright lights. It's cold – we don't know what cold is but it is different to how it was, different to what we were used to. There is light for the first time! And noise! So many new noises and so much louder than we are used to. Is it any wonder that babies cry when they are born?

And so from the very beginning we start to protect ourselves from this strange new world and in doing so we become less open. Every interaction we have with our world and the people in it encourages us to stay open and loving or close up a little bit more and defend ourselves. By the time many of us are adults we carry 'emotional baggage' with us that affects us a little or a lot depending on our experiences. Sometimes, as a protection from being hurt, we don't let others get too close. We may in fact never find the level of love and openness we started with unless we work consciously to face our fears and face life with an open heart. Thankfully, when we die many of the protective layers that we have placed around ourselves during our lifetime are released and we are able to love more deeply than we ever felt possible while in earthly existence.

The absence of a physical body also makes it easier for loved ones to come into our space and flow love to us. In this way, loved ones who have passed over truly do feel more love for us after they die. They can love completely as Brian felt he was now able to do.

Brian had not had any more or less emotional baggage than most of us, but after death he was completely open. It was wonderful for me to experience how he was enjoying feeling even closer to his wife and daughter, how many of his barriers to loving and feeling love had fallen away along with his physical body when he died. Following the communication from Brian, his wife and daughter both now knew that their sensing him around them wasn't just wishful thinking; he was really with them, watching over them and that was a wonderful feeling to have. No matter what they faced in life he would be there, as would his love and support for them. Neither of them would have to face anything alone again.

Mother and daughter left very happy, the daughter saying I had made Mum's year. I was glad the daughter had stayed and persisted in her efforts and refused to leave; she clearly had her father's spirit with her pushing her on. I reflected on how often in common speech we do talk about people having a loved one's spirit with them. Perhaps the expression was closer to reality than many people realised! I smiled to myself. The daughter's determination and firm resolve had resulted in a special moment for all of us. It was one I will always treasure.

Starting Out

It often seems to me that I have had two lives this lifetime: the first as a bank manager working for Lloyds Bank, living a materialistic life and not really thinking for myself, and the second questioning everything I thought I knew, searching for answers and developing natural abilities I never even dreamed I had. My life now is altogether more fabulous. I feel alive. I am in my life for the first time, actively and consciously creating my future, playing my part. I love what I do, demonstrating mediumship to large groups, showing thousands of people that there is no death, easing their pain and awakening them to a new, more empowering way of looking at life. I am often asked how I developed the confidence to do what I now do. To most it seems like a colossal leap from learning about the spiritual side of life to sharing that knowledge with hundreds of people at a time and in front of television cameras. How was it that I could make such incredible changes in my life and so quickly? As I look back on my life it seems that everything that happened to me had been significant and that one step naturally and effortlessly led to the next. All I had to do was to step forward into the opportunities that presented themselves and do my best.

Previously, I had spent nine years developing my psychic abilities and spiritual understandings. Five of these had been in the UK, working as a healer and medium and the latter four in New Zealand. During this time, I initially committed myself to family life, which meant there were only limited opportunities to practice as a medium. I missed the mediumship, the healing and my UK clients but I was kept busy with two young children, just 17 months apart. However, there continued to be no end of spiritual insights and I realised that 'what' I did was not as important as 'how' I did it. This spiritual perspective helped me to give my best at whatever I turned my hand to and affirmed that I was doing the right thing for me at the right time. As a new mother I was learning about love and compassion on an entirely different level and although I did not realise it then, it helped my mediumship in precisely the way it needed developing.

Once both my children were settled into kindergarten I felt an inner stirring to begin using my abilities to help people once more. This was confirmed on a physical level by people who had lost loved ones to spirit world

14

starting to find me even though I was not advertising and only a couple of people, my partner Andrew and his mother Mary, knew about my mediumship abilities. The trickle of clients grew into a steady flow and in no time at all I found myself asking internally to be given an opportunity to practise my mediumship in front of a group again, as I had done in the UK. I wanted to develop my abilities further because people have a right to know that there is no death. I have a responsibility to share what I know and that responsibility lies more heavily on me because of the abilities I have. Within two weeks of my internal request, not one but two opportunities arose to speak to groups and demonstrate mediumship. Speakers I had booked for the spiritual centre I was part of and for the local spiritualist church cancelled, and so I had to organise replacement speakers for both groups at very short notice. I did not want to let either group down, but where could I find someone of quality at such short notice? As the days of the talks loomed closer, no suitable speakers had been found. I came to the conclusion that the universe was giving *me* the opportunity I had asked for. It was time to take another leap of faith, though I did so tentatively at first. I put my own name forward as a substitute speaker with a suggested topic of mediumship and did not have to wait long for a response. Both groups accepted my suggestion enthusiastically and overnight the small step of putting my name forward became a giant leap. Inside, I knew it was time to take it.

My first demonstration was at the spiritual centre I belonged to and in no time at all the day arrived and I was there in front of the group. My heart was racing and I did my best to breathe deeply so that I would at least appear calm on the outside. I took a moment or two to scan the room. Attendance was good; about 45 people had crammed into the meeting room. Many were curious to see how good I was and the demonstration was an easy way for them to check me out. I was grateful to see familiar faces in the audience as it relaxed me to be among friends, although I was still a little apprehensive. It had been at least five years since my last public demonstration in the UK so I knew I was likely to be a little rusty doing mediumship in front of this group. In my head the same question was repeating itself: What if nothing happens and I can't see or sense spirit beings? I told myself to trust and to work as I did when I was one-to-one with people; the rest would flow. I was also unsure about how a New Zealand audience would react to me and how I would get on managing the group energies.

My lack of recent practice and Andrew, my kiwi partner, coming to see me in action for the first time were more than enough to make me nervous, but I also knew I had a lot riding on the evening for other reasons. What no one else knew at that time was that I had been guided to start a new kind of school in New Zealand. I was also shown that the money for the development of the school was to come primarily through me sharing what I knew by doing mediumship shows – this was due to happen in the next few years. If the mediumship didn't go well, where was I going to raise the kind of money required to create a new choice in education? This concept of an alternative educational choice had been conveyed to me recently and linked back to a message or teaching I received at the time of my spiritual awakening some years previously: that I was here for the children, to help them 'keep their lights on'. I felt a huge responsibility to do my best.

I started the show by introducing myself and explaining that this was an opportunity for me to demonstrate in front of a 'safe' group what I could already do in private with individuals. Eyes looked back at me and there was the odd smile. I smiled back. I asked for their help. If I gave them a message they had to be completely honest with me and let me know what I was getting right and what I wasn't. I had learned from my time as a trainer working for Lloyds Bank that one of the best ways to get better at something is to ask for feedback. By doing this, you learn quickly what you are getting right and what you aren't and you can ther use this information to refine what you are doing. Receiving feedback is a way of accelerating your learning but when you first do it, it can take you right out of your comfort zone.

I settled myself in a chair at the front of the room and closed my eyes for a few moments to calm myself. The questions returned in my head. How would spirit world guide me to the right people? Would they work differently here in New Zealand than they did in the UK? Would Maori ancestors in particular be happy to work with me, or would they only want to use their own people? I allowed the questions in my mind to subside and concentrated on being open to receiving a sign in whatever way it came. I was open to a light, an image, a sound, or a feeling.

It came as a feeling. Somewhere in my heart centre there was a pull towards an older lady in the audience. I asked if she would like to join me at the front of the group. By separating her from the group I reasoned I would have more chance of separating her loved ones in spirit from the spirits of others in the room. She was happy to oblige and came forward to join me in the seats at the front. I calmed myself again, taking a few longer, deeper breaths. I put my awareness into the core of my being and then into the lady's space. I sensed a man and a woman in spirit world with her: her mother and her father. I communicated that I had both of her parents with me. I knew that the audience would not be surprised by this information, given her age, and I also dismissed the inner critic in my head, knowing there'd be more convincing proof to come. I then linked more strongly with the lady's father and the hairs on my arms stood on end. This was so obvious that all those sitting nearby could see. For me this has become a significant sign that my link is strong and the information or message is absolutely accurate. Her father gave me his name which I passed on. The name was correct. I was able to relax a little. It was beginning to come back. The lady's father explained the circumstances of his death, which I relayed and again the lady confirmed the information as correct. The communication with her father had brought back pleasant memories for her and she was very happy with the level of proof I had been able to give her. It was a good start. I remembered from my time in the UK that often the first link is the hardest. I reassured myself that the links should get easier from here on in.

They did and they didn't. Some links were better than others. A young man called John came through for a younger audience member. He was her brother and had died very tragically. I received something about a note he left her. I couldn't quite make out what he meant but knew it wasn't a suicide note. It turned out to be a poem he had written to her. The girl had brought the poem with her that evening and that was what John had been talking about. She read it out to the group. There was a lot of love between them. The girl here still dearly missed her brother but after his message was better able to accept and understand his decision to be on the spirit side of life. It is so important sometimes just to know that our loved ones are alright, particularly if they were emotionally troubled or depressed before passing. It gives great comfort to know that they are at last at peace.

The evening had had a promising start but I recognised that I wasn't up to the standard I had been in the UK. None of the messages had been 'wrong' as such, they were just a little vague. I was used to getting everything correct and felt I would need some more practice to get up to my previous standard. Whilst I was disappointed, Andrew, along with several others, couldn't believe what they had seen. They had no idea that I could bring through messages to the skill level and accuracy I did. I had no shortage of requests for private consultations. My diary was filled for weeks ahead so I would get ample practice one-to-one, but I knew I needed more practice with large groups and was pleased that on the following Sunday I would be giving the demonstration at the local spiritualist church. On Sunday, the audience would be one I was not familiar with and so I would be stepping out of my comfort zone just that little bit further.

On the afternoon of the demonstration I was washing the dishes when I was told internally to make sure that I worked from my heart centre and not my head when I attended the spiritualist church later that evening. Normally my guidance comes through when I meditate or I may 'receive' the information in a dream. If I fail to meditate then I 'receive' messages at other times; generally when I am doing something mundane such as washing dishes. What I make sure I do is *listen*. I recognise these messages as guidance as they just pop into my mind. I may be thinking about something completely different or nothing much at all and all of a sudden there is a complete thought in my head. It stands out against my other thoughts. It has a simple truth to it but I don't remember consciously thinking it. As Einstein once said 'when the solution is simple, God is answering'.

The demonstration was my first visit to the local spiritualist church. I had only ever attended a spiritualist church once before at the beginning of my spiritual searching, in the UK. Being a 'church', they had a structured format with hymns and prayers, very much like a regular church but instead of a sermon there is a demonstration of mediumship. I was invited to talk about myself and my philosophy for about 20 minutes and then demonstrate mediumship for 20 minutes. I reasoned that if I was attending a spiritualist church meeting I would want messages rather than philosophy. I wasn't very sure of their protocol but when the time came they seemed such a very friendly and open group that I felt comfortable asking them what they wanted at the start of my session. As I expected, they agreed they would much rather have messages. My talk about myself was very brief and probably it was just as well, as I hadn't really worked out how to express my philosophy at that time. Even today my philosophy continues to evolve as I evolve.

I must have relayed about eight different messages; all were happily received and understood. Neither the audience nor I wanted the messages to end and when I did overrun no one seemed to mind. The feedback I received later was that I was the best medium they had seen in years. I was flattered by the feedback of course but my analytical, critical side had to ask myself why. Why was I perceived as being better than people who presumably had demonstrated mediumship much longer than I had? I was still a novice in many respects. Was it because I didn't go to a section of the audience asking if someone could 'take a John', but went to an individual and engaged directly with them? Perhaps they hadn't seen anyone work like that before. Yet going to the specific individual was my natural way of working. If the spirit and the person here are linked by love I am drawn to them – I cannot help but know who it is I am to go to. It puzzled me that other mediums worked differently. Perhaps this was one of the reasons I had been guided to learn in my own way, away from the spiritualist church's more traditional methodology. I didn't know but certainly the way I worked had been very well received.

There was one more opportunity for me to demonstrate mediumship at the spiritual centre I belonged to before I was guided to organise a mediumship show for the general public. I was guided to do this as soon as possible and – surprise, surprise – I was washing the dishes when I 'knew' that this was what I had to do.

As well as raising money for an alternative school, I was shown that through my mediumship I could also assist in the campaign against genetic engineering and raise local awareness of the dangers of genetic engineering. At the time the government had just lifted the moratorium on the release of GE organisms into the New Zealand food chain so the need to get finance together and inform people was immediate. This meant the public shows needed to be scheduled earlier than I had first intended. Mediumship and genetic engineering perhaps seem strange bed partners initially but not when you look at genetic engineering from a spiritual perspective. I was shown the shows as a choice, not told what to do – it was a way that I could help if I chose to. It wasn't a difficult choice to make and without hesitation I booked a hotel room for the Sunday evening and by the Thursday we had sold out all 200 tickets. The fact that the tickets sold out so quickly and effortlessly gave me confidence that it was 'meant to be' and also showed me that the earlier audiences had been happy with the standard of my mediumship and that word had got around.

In the beginning I was nervous about doing a show to a large audience but I helped myself to overcome this by focusing on what the shows were about. The shows are first and foremost about love, showing people that there is no death, giving proof of survival beyond reasonable doubt, even if individual members of the audience do not receive a message personally. If I can do this I can reduce the fear and hurt that many people are feeling here on the earth plane. I learned to focus on the audience and their feelings rather than my own, and in that way I no longer felt my nervousness. The show is primarily about the audience and their loved ones in spirit, not about me. I am simply the go-between – the 'medium'. For me, the shows are a way of extending myself and my mediumship so that it reaches the highest possible level and about helping people understand that they too can talk to their loved ones in spirit world. Communication does not always need to be through a medium. What I do can be learned if you would *love* to. So the shows are about sharing all that I know – by demonstration and by teaching. I hope that the shows remind the audience about their own eternal nature and leave those attending feeling inspired and uplifted, having connected with their loved ones.

The story of that first show is told in my book, *Medium Rare*. On that night my mediumship really came together and was more to the standard I had known in the UK. The show was very well received. Many people had seen nothing like it before and I had further requests for private readings. I was delighted with how well the show had gone, as the level of mediumship was better than anything I had ever experienced. When I was told internally that I was at 75% of my potential as a medium I was thrilled but I could see there was still scope to get significantly better and that was what I wanted to do.

More shows followed and both Andrew and I were overwhelmed by their popularity. We often had to go back to areas quite soon to meet the demand for tickets. Soon we would have covered all the places we could easily travel to. If we wanted to keep going with the shows it would mean going on tour and this would mean Andrew giving up his job and the children not going to kindergarten during that time. It was a big decision for all of us and it took us several weeks to make but it is one we have never regretted. In the meantime, we continued with shows closer to home. There was still much for me to learn.

Learning requires growth – expansion into new areas, areas you may not feel entirely comfortable in, exploring new ideas about how things are and not being afraid to say 'I do not know'. Learning can be scary but without it there is no growth, there is only stagnation. In the words of Helen Keller 'life is either a daring adventure or nothing at all!'.

My challenge to the universe was to assist me to improve my standard of mediumship to a higher level than anything I had seen or heard of before. In turn I agreed to be open to learn and to push back my own boundaries at every opportunity. I agreed to dare to be all that I could be. To live my truth, not just keep it to myself.

A 'New' Kind of Mediumship

When I look back now, I can say that soon after my very first experience of seeing spirits at the Neuro Linguistic Programming course in Regents College I knew within me that one day I would be working on stage as a medium to large audiences. At the time, however, it was as though I almost played a game with myself, constantly asking if that was what I was here to do, and in my heart of hearts knowing that was what I would *love* to do. I hardly dared believe that I would have such ability or be given so much responsibility. I think that many of us know deep down inside what we would love to do with and in our lives; we do know why we are here, but hardly dare even admit it to ourselves, much less other people. I guess my story of how I came to do what I now do is the story of someone who 'dared to believe'.

I believe that anyone who would love to do mediumship work can develop their natural ability to do so. I am not particularly 'special'. It is the love of the work and my curiosity for finding out the 'truth' about this reality that opens the door between the different dimensions. I believe that one of the reasons why I had to have my own varied and wide-ranging experiences while developing as a medium is so that in time I can share what I know with people who would like to learn. Mediumship is not 'rocket science'; it is about love. It is about physically, emotionally, mentally and spiritually clearing yourself as a channel so that you can pass on messages and insights with as few of your own misconceptions, prejudices and limiting beliefs contaminating the messages as possible. You have to get your own beliefs and ego out of the way in the same way you do when giving healing. For this reason, I consider that my mediumship has helped my healing and my healing has helped my mediumship.

People often ask me: Why would anyone want to talk to dead people? It is because they aren't cold dead bodies – they are just like you and me on the inside. They have thoughts, feelings and usually more understanding than we do about why certain things are happening in our lives. Also, the love that I experience while communicating with them is phenomenal. It is very similar to the loving state I experience while giving or receiving healing. In addition, the messages loved ones have for us can be profound, with applications not just for the individual but also for the whole audience, and sometimes the whole of humanity. This emotional and moving story is a superb illustration of this.

A strong pull from Spirit led me to stand in front of a dark-haired woman sitting towards the back of the room. As I stood connecting with her loved ones I wasn't really sure she wanted a message but her loved ones in spirit had other ideas. I could sense her mother and father and the atmosphere between the daughter and parents felt strained, to say the least. I looked at the lady in the audience and she looked back at me. I decided to test the water. "I have what feels like your mother and father with me." The lady nodded and although she didn't look at me, I handed her a microphone.

An overwhelming sense of remorse flooded my body. "Mum is so sorry that she allowed what happened to go on," I conveyed. The father spirit was standing back with his head down, an indication of shame. More remorse flowed from Mum. Oh, how she wished she had done more. My own thoughts raced immediately to sexual abuse but then I found myself shaking my head. "No, that wasn't what was meant," I was told very firmly. Instead, I was shown physical abuse, the girl being beaten black and blue. I could see that Dad was the perpetrator, hence his shame, and Mum was there but didn't intervene. She hadn't stopped him – something she always deeply regretted when she was here. The woman didn't really need to say anything. Her face showed that it was all true, but she quietly confirmed that what I had seen was the truth.

Next, Mum showed me a door with a coat hook on it. A coat hook? It didn't make sense. So I described what I was seeing to the woman: "Mum is showing me a door with a coat hook on it. Do you know why she would do that?" She nodded and somehow found the strength to explain: "My dad used to hang me on the door hook when I was naughty." A ripple ran through the audience and we all felt for what she had been through.

"You have done well," came the message from spirit world for the woman. "You have learned that your past does not create your future and you have not let this incident affect you as much as it might have done." Spirit told me to ask her what she did now. I wasn't quite sure where it was leading but knew to trust. "I am being told to ask you what work you do now because it is significant." Again, the lady nodded. "I work with abused children," came the response. She had turned an extremely negative situation into something positive – she had used her life to transform anger directed at her into love, patience and compassion for others. There was much admiration and support for her from spirit world and from the audience. It was humbling to meet someone who had achieved so much from such a difficult starting point.

On a personal level, the woman now knew her Mum was remorseful about what had happened and felt closure because of this. Additionally, the lesson for all who were present was that when 'bad' things happen in our lives they can actually inspire us to do 'good' things – to reach within ourselves and be the best that we can be, despite the situation.

As I developed my abilities and understandings I came to understand that the time was right for a 'new' kind of mediumship, for humanity collectively and for me personally – a mediumship that went beyond the traditional methodology of symbolic messages. I realised my messages as well as helping individuals could also have profound and wide-ranging applications or teachings for humanity in general, as the example just described did. To do this, the information communicated needed to be increasingly accurate and beyond my possible knowing. This was crystallised for me several years ago when I bought a book called *The New Mediumship* by a lady called Grace Cooke. When I got it home I already had two other copies of the same book on my bookshelf. Initially I kicked myself. Why hadn't I recognised the title as one I already had? I had bought the second book thinking I was buying a different book as it had a different cover to the first.

However, then buying a third copy of the same book with the same cover as the second book seemed more than a 'reasonable mistake'. What was the universe trying to tell me? I read the book from cover to cover, not once but twice. It did not tell me anything I did not already know. Why then did I have to buy a third copy of it? Sometime later I realised that whilst I totally understood that the time was right for a 'new' kind of mediumship, I didn't know how it worked and I'd been trying to find a book that explained it. Buying the book three times showed me that it was something that I *really* wanted to do but that there was no book to explain it. I had to find it out for *myself*.

It is still an evolving process but let me explain what I *now* understand is the key difference between the traditional and the 'new' kind of mediumship. A medium working using the traditional method is shown symbols, which they then have to interpret to pass on a message. If Spirit shows five fingers it means five, but five what? Is it five years since they passed over? Did they live at No. 5? Was their birthday in the fifth month or on the fifth of the month? Only through experience has this particular symbol become self-explanatory for me: five fingers usually symbolises five children. It may be five children in spirit world or it may mean that they had five children. Fingers are used by my guides to symbolise flesh and blood. My guides

32

know how I think and so this suits my way of working, but fingers may not represent children to all mediums.

When a number is just shown as a digit, it is harder to interpret. For example, a young man in spirit world, the son of the lady I was on stage with, showed me the number 20. Internally, I had asked him what he meant and he just showed me 20 again. So I had to get his mother to help me interpret it. "Your son keeps showing me a number 20. I know it is significant. Can you explain why he would do that?" The lady knew at once and explained that her son had died on the 20th. It was very significant to her. She was happy with the information. To her it was enough proof, but I am always questioning and wanting to be given more detail. Why can I 'receive' 20 and not 20th? Why couldn't he give me 20th and the month? I still don't know. I have learned that life is an ongoing experience, a playful interaction with an incredible universe that wants us to understand more about ourselves and what is possible here. When I find something I can't do, for whatever reason, I ask to be shown how to do it – knowing that if it is right for me, all will be revealed. We need to keep asking the questions and pushing back the boundaries of what is possible and the universe will find a way. Perhaps I will find out in time for my next book!

Symbols are very useful to a medium as these examples and more throughout the book show.

You can work at being more and more accurate in interpreting them but they do have a *downside*. If you don't interpret the symbol accurately a sceptic may say that you are being too vague or general, and if you interpret what you are seeing wrongly the message is perceived as being incorrect. Spirit have worked with me increasingly over the years to develop new and better ways of communicating – the 'new' kind of mediumship. I have now learned to be more open and have developed the ability to receive all information on all channels, in whatever way is most suitable. Increasingly, communications have taken the form of feelings or simply 'knowing' something as a whole new concept rather than building it up from the traditional, small, symbolic parts, which have then to be interpreted.

One of my earliest experiences of this 'new' mediumship was in the UK. I was doing a private party for a group of people where each guest came to see me individually to have a reading while the others were in a separate room. When it came time to talk to one of the guests who was particularly sceptical about my abilities, I was feeling quite nervous. When someone is sceptical their energy field is quite closed and it can be difficult to 'receive' information for them. I needn't have worried. Clairvoyantly I knew that the lady had very nearly lost her daughter, aged two. When I revealed this the lady's mouth fell open and I could feel her wondering how I knew this. After her initial shock I felt she rationalised it by thinking that someone else in the group had told me. She asked defiantly, "What did she nearly die of?" I knew she was just checking me out, testing to see if I was for real.

"A twisted colon," tripped out of my mouth before I had time to think. I saw it all clearly – no symbols, no interpretation required. The words had come straight out of my mouth, seemingly not running through my mind first, and I just *knew* it was correct. I would have staked my life on it. The accuracy of the information clearly took the lady by surprise and she was very attentive for the rest of her session. By the end of the evening she had interrogated the others attending to make sure they had not told me about her daughter. None of them had. As a result, she had a lot more questions for me before I left that evening. She was no longer a sceptic!

The 'new' mediumship does not require the medium to interpret and so there is less chance of error – ideas, concepts and thoughts are conveyed as complete knowings. Over the years I have developed straightforward techniques to make it easier to 'receive' such communications. It has taken a great deal of practice with many different people here and in spirit world. I still receive many of my messages in the traditional symbolic form but more and more they are coming through simply as 'knowings'.

The Shows

At the shows I generally find that there is something like five or six loved ones in spirit for each person physically present in the audience. So for a physical audience of two hundred people there could be well over one thousand spirits. That makes for a very full room! It takes a lot of energy and concentration to keep other spirits at bay while I identify which spirits are with a particular individual and then work out which are the most important links for that person. I don't want to spend time talking to the next door neighbour if Mum has just passed over. Unless, of course, they were having an affair with the next door neighbour! Seriously, though I may see affairs I do not talk of them at the shows. The audience has to feel relaxed for me to be able to do what I do and if they felt that information such as this may be discussed they would be on edge. For similar reasons, I do not talk about terminations as they are the private decisions of the individuals concerned and so I refer to them as either babies who did not make it onto the earth plane or miscarriages.

I do not choose the people I go to. I am guided to them predominantly by a feeling in the middle of my chest, I'm almost pulled like a magnet but it feels more emotional, more love-based. My feet just take me in the general direction and then they just stop. I stand very still and look across the row of people sensing, using my heart centre in the middle of my chest, where I am most drawn to. As a child I used to pay a parlour game called *Hunt the Thimble* with other children. The aim was to find a small thimble that was not visible by following the guidance of someone, usually an adult or older child who knew where the thimble was hidden. If you moved closer to the spot you would be told you were getting warmer, and if you got really close, that you were getting really hot. Finding my links as a medium is a lot like that game, except the sensation I feel is a loving energy flow or connection rather than heat.

Whom I link with at each particular show is orchestrated by my guides: invisible helpers that I sense working with me. I ask them to lead me to the most appropriate links so that by the end of the night, even if a person has not received a message themselves, the quality of evidence that I have given to the others is such that they can still go away knowing that there is an afterlife, that we are eternal. I am led to the people

I can best get a link with; they may not always be the people who most need or want a message. If there is still too much emotion around a particular passing it can make meaningful communication difficult or if a person is too nervous or is desperately willing a particular person through that also can stop me being able to talk to their loved ones. 'Desire' energy can work against us with spirit communication in the same way that it can work against us in other areas of our lives. In Buddhism one of the core beliefs is that 'desire is the cause of all suffering' and with good reason. When we really want something to happen we create a pull energy and this type of energy can block us from receiving what it is we want. Don't take my word for it though, reflect upon your own experience of life when you really, really wanted something to happen, when you really, really wanted to date that special someone, pass that test, lose weight – could you?

I have learned that to attract the events, people and situations I most want or need, I must be relaxed and open, and in a state of knowing that what I most want or need *is* coming. If I am not open to receive, it can't come. Spirit communication works in much the same way; our loved ones are with us all the time, it was they who inspire us to come to the shows (we only think it is our idea), so all we need do is be fully present, relaxed, send them love and leave the rest to them.

I ask that loved ones come through with loving messages and share happy and humorous memories to help lighten the whole show as the subject matter is usually emotionally charged enough. Loved ones can provide humorous memories as evidence to show that it is them, as well as sad. At one show, spirit world had clearly taken my request for humour seriously. Passing along a row of dimly lit chairs to find my next link with an audience member I suddenly found myself carefully stepping over chickens. The audience's giggles at my apparently strange and unexplained behaviour brought me sharply into the present. I had only been half aware of what I was doing. My rational left brain clicked in. I was in a theatre for goodness sake, there couldn't be any chickens between the seats! But of course, they were spirit world chickens! My rational left brain was not too impressed, but before I could give it too much thought I immediately had my next link, a grandmother, for the lady at my side. "Can you understand why your grandmother would be coming through from spirit world with chickens?" I asked.

"Grandmother kept chickens and they did run around my feet when I went to visit," she remembered. "I had to step over them, just like you did," she laughed. "Marigolds" popped into my head and I immediately thought of a brand of household rubber gloves that are popular in the UK. I couldn't yet see the connection between rubber gloves and chickens. Grandmother was laughing and it was all very funny judging by the audience's response. I realised I was still stepping over invisible chickens. "Is there a link with Marigolds and your grandmother?" I asked, dodging yet another chook. "No. But she did grow chrysanthemums," came the response. The grandaughter was thinking flowers and I was thinking rubber gloves. I realised that the Marigold brand of rubber gloves is not sold in New Zealand so I explained that in the UK Marigold is a brand of rubber gloves. Suddenly I saw what grandmother meant. "Your grandmother is laughing about you wearing rubber gloves to stuff a chicken when you were younger." The lady remembered the time well and the thought of wearing rubber gloves to stuff a chicken brought another wave of laughter from the audience. The link was a new experience for me as I had never seen spirit world chickens before; I had seen dogs, cats and horses and other birds occasionally but never a chicken. It certainly brightened the evening by lifting the emotions.

When I link with an audience member I can either work with them sitting in the audience or invite them to join me on stage. The latter is preferable as it shows a clear intent to all other spirits present that for the next few minutes I will only be linking with spirits linked to the one person I take on stage. The physical distance between us and the rest of the audience also seems to help. It also means that the audience can clearly see and hear the response from the person, to the messages I give them. Sometimes, the person reacts in a non-verbal way or they forget to talk into the microphone; if they are on stage the rest of the audience can see that the message is being accepted. That is important because, as hard as I try to get messages through to as many people as possible, there are those who will not receive a message themselves and I want them to see how accurate the messages are. I don't take everyone on stage though. If I feel that it would be physically difficult for the audience member to get on stage or it would make the person too nervous I let them remain seated in the audience. If they get too nervous I may not be able to maintain the link to the desired standard and in the end it is more important that they are relaxed and that the message does get through.

When I first establish a link I start talking to the person in spirit world and passing on information from them to the person here. As I do, the link with them gets stronger. I believe it is because I pay them attention that the link strengthens in this way. When the link is really strong the hairs on my arms stand on end and at that point it is time to take that person up on stage. It is funny; I didn't much like the long blonde hairs on my arms as I was growing up but now I find them invaluable. They confirm the connection for me and also provide visible evidence to the audience that something is happening. They stand on end even when the room is very warm. Audience members nearby often report experiencing a similar effect or feel a shudder going down their spines.

As I have done mediumship shows and become more experienced, my understanding of the different aspects of working with a large audience has developed. There are so many variables with the potential to unsettle an audience or me and many things that can appear to 'go wrong'. I remember one particular show where I had difficulty getting a message accepted by a lady.

I was about halfway through a show when the spirits around a middle-aged lady pulled me to her. First I felt her mother Sarah, a quietly spoken soul, who had passed about five years previously.

"I can sense your mother's spirit with you," I said. "Is it about five years now since she passed over?"

"Just about," came the reply.

"She tells me her name is Sarah. Sarah with an H."

"Yes that's right." The lady's eyes lit up.

Sarah showed me that she had her brother with her in spirit world and I explained what I was seeing. "Your mother is showing me that she has her brother with her and that he passed long before she did, that he was just a young man when he died." Try as I might

I couldn't get his name and so I moved on to how Mum and her brother had passed. The details were confirmed as correct. Then I went on to relay a clear message from Mum to her daughter, about her three children. "Mum says your three children now need to be brought together."

"No, I don't understand that," she said. "I only have two children." I was taken aback. "Are *you* one of three children?" I enquired. I knew that wasn't exactly what I had heard but thought perhaps I had been mistaken and the message was about her and her siblings, not her own children. Perhaps she was one of the children that needed to be brought together. "No, there are four of us," she replied.

I was puzzled. The communication at the beginning had been very clear and accurate and this part had also seemed as clear. It had come from the same place within me and from the same spirit as the rest of the communication. When I am talking to several spirits they all hold their consciousness in a different place within me so that I can sense that there is more than one and separate what they each individually want to say. This message was definitely from the same spirit.

"You didn't lose a child?" I enquired, trying the original tack. "No," came the quick response. I decided to move on and not pursue it. Occasionally messages don't make sense, usually because I am interpreting them wrongly, but this one had seemed straightforward. I wasn't sure how I could have misinterpreted it. I let it go and moved on. The rest of the message and information I passed on to the lady was accepted as correct.

I thought no more of it until the end of the show when she asked to see me privately. When I saw her she could not apologise enough. She explained that she did have three children. Her first child, a girl, had been illegitimate and had been adopted at birth. The woman had been very young at the time, a child herself and too young to be a mother. Some of her own family did not know about the baby and she did not want to say anything during the show in case word got back to family members, through someone in the audience, before she had time to explain. She fully appreciated that now it was time to tell them. Mum's message, that all her children needed to be 'brought together', had got through.

What a relief! I was not used to messages not being accepted and it was good to get the confirmation that the message had in fact been correct. I fully understood the sensitive and difficult position she had been in. If my link is clear, evidenced by the hairs on my arms standing on end and the clarity of the information, I know to stand my ground to an extent, but I also know not to make a big thing out of it and make the recipient

45

of the message uncomfortable. I treat people in the way I would like to be treated and recognise that they can have their own reasons for not accepting a correct message, as this lady had. It's nice to have a mystery solved for my own satisfaction even if it is after the show. The disappointing thing is that other audience members don't get to hear the 'real or complete story' and may go away not fully convinced with the information I have brought through.

When I was less experienced a message not being accepted would really knock my confidence, but nowadays I understand that there can be a variety of reasons for a message not being accepted. Sometimes people genuinely don't know the names of their ancestors or the details about them I bring through. Sometimes it takes a while for them to understand the message and sometimes there are more personal reasons, as in the previous story and in the following one.

It was towards the end of a show, within the final 10 minutes, that I stopped in front of a lady a few rows back from the front. We looked at each other for a moment or two and then I felt a gentleman in front of her – he came in with half a wedding ring. To me it was clear that he was her husband – half a wedding ring usually means one partner is in spirit world and one is still here. He was just a bit taller than me and he presented himself in a United States Air Force uniform.

I described the wedding ring and the uniform and asked if she had lost a partner to spirit world who was in the Air Force. "No," came the adamant response. I was baffled. He was standing there as clear as day in his uniform. Was it that I was getting tired, I wondered? "You haven't lost a brother-in-law who was in the Air Force and whose wife is still here?" I asked quite bewildered. "No," came the definite reply again. I moved on to the gentleman next to her, passing on a message that made perfect sense to him. I checked to see if he knew the man in the uniform in case I'd got the two people confused but no, he didn't know the gentleman I was describing either. It wasn't until the end of the show that all was revealed. The lady's friend came to speak to me privately. She was upset and apologised on her friend's behalf. The man in the US Air Force uniform had been her friend's second husband but her friend hadn't wanted to talk to him as she had only ever loved her first husband! He was who she hoped to speak to. The sad part was that had she let her second husband come through he would have probably stood to one side and let her first husband come through after him. By rejecting the initial link she had shut out that possibility and I had given up and moved to the man next to her.

Sometimes, a message isn't accepted because I am at fault: either I have interpreted what I am seeing

47

incorrectly or with too narrow a view. A lovely example of this was in the UK when I first started working as a psychic. Using my clairvoyant vision I saw one lady looking at a red brick wall.

"Do you feel like you are hitting your head against a brick wall?" I asked.

'No," she said quite bemused by the question.

"Have you hit a block of some kind then?"

"No," she repeated.

I decided to explain what I was seeing; it is usually the best strategy. "All I can see is red brick," I explained.

"I've been cleaning my kitchen floor," she said.

I thought she was just being helpful, some people are. "No," I said, "it's not a kitchen floor. This is red brick. It must mean something." I struggled on, but all I could see internally was red brick. Was I the one with the block, was that what it meant? Surely I would just see nothing at all, if I was blocked.

Gently, the lady took my hand to get my attention.

"It is my kitchen floor," she said quietly. "My kitchen floor is red brick and I have been on my hands and knees for the last three days red-leading it."

At last, what I was seeing made sense. I could move on to a new piece of information.

The way spirit world seem to communicate is that they give you a piece of information and as soon as it is understood they give you the next piece. If what I say is inaccurate or misleading, they keep showing me the same symbol/image until the person and I understand the true meaning. However, I cannot afford to get stuck with a piece of information for too long and so I have learned to take back a piece of information if it can't be understood and that then opens up the flow of information again. Nine times out of ten Spirit then give me the 'stuck' piece of information in a different way and I am able to unravel it.

Receiving messages from spirit world the traditional way is a lot like playing Pictionary, the game where someone draws a picture and you have to guess what it is they are drawing. Some people you play with only have to draw two or three lines and you immediately get what they are drawing – you are on their wavelength. Other pictures you simply cannot guess at all; even when you know what it is they have drawn, you still cannot see it! Receiving information from spirits is a lot like that. Some are on your wavelength and some aren't.

Because of this, sometimes to make sense of a message I have to think outside the square and so do the people receiving the message. One lady I recall was able to accept all the information I gave her from her deceased family members, except the name Harold. Her father who was with me in spirit form could not believe she did not remember Harold. "You know

49

Harold – you must remember Harold," he kept urging. The poor lady's face was a complete blank.

"Harold's here too," said Dad, but still the lady couldn't place the name. All I could add was that he felt big. I couldn't see a person or a face, just that he was huge almost like two people.

"He's big!" I said, which seemingly didn't help the lady at all. Dad was laughing in my head. I was glad he could see the funny side. I left her to think about it and moved on. Midway through the next message she laughed out loud and called out, "I know who Harold is. He was my nana's horse. We would ride him when we went to visit." Why hadn't Dad just shown me a horse? Perhaps it adds to the entertainment of the shows? Who knows! I can only think that he felt like two people to me because at some level I was sensing his four legs and his size.

Sometimes, what initially seems the most obvious meaning of a message proves to be incorrect. The information given to me can be completely clear and correct but when I try to make sense of it through my own memory bank, I end up with something completely different to what a loved one in spirit world intended to convey. It is not until you understand the complete picture more fully that the message becomes clear.

This sad story of an unsung hero illustrates this clearly.

A young man in spirit world took me to his sister and mum in the audience. I invited them on stage and I could see that they had come prepared. The sister held an old worn teddy bear that had clearly been much loved in its day and his mum had a lock of blonde hair. They settled themselves in the chairs on stage and I suspected that the audience was preparing themselves emotionally for a child to come through. The teddy bear was a real giveaway. There were tears in Mum's and sister's eyes before the message had even started and I could feel that the audience's hearts were with them. It is heartwarming for me to experience the love and compassion that audiences have for each other at the shows. It gives me hope for our future that we can and do feel for each other in this way.

I didn't have a child with me though, I had a grown man of about 30. I needed to make this clear right from the start to the ladies on stage with me and to the audience. "I have a young man, your son with me," I said, directing myself to Mum. Mum confirmed that yes, her son had been 28 when he died. The teddy and the hair were his; they were family 'treasures' that had been kept for a long time. "This is your brother," I indicated, this time directing myself to the young lady. She nodded but was too tearful to speak. I took the lock of hair I had been offered and held it in my hand to help strengthen the connection. Instantly, I felt a sudden massive impact. It came straight on, almost taking my breath away. "There was a massive impact," I explained when I could catch my breath. "Head on." Mum and sister could only nod agreement. Tears flowed freely down their faces and I could see that it would not be easy for them to speak.

I went back to the flow of information, communicating with the brother in spirit world. I was holding a steering wheel; my physical hands and arms were out in front of me modelling the action. The audience looked on, spellbound. My hands were gripping so tightly to the wheel that my knuckles were almost white. The steering wheel was going all over the place. With my psychic vision I could see only white in front of me. Absolutely everything was white. My memory banks scanned through all my memories. What did this mean? The only thing I could connect it with was driving a car on ice when it is out of control in a skid.

"Did he skid in a car on ice?" I asked.

"No," his mum said, looking at me anxiously. Perhaps I wasn't really connecting with her son. I could almost see the thought go through her head. She had so wanted a message from her son. "He wasn't in a car," she went on. I was shocked and the audience was shocked too. I was sitting there with my arms outstretched gripping a steering wheel – it had to be a car. I really didn't want to get this one 'wrong'; the emotions were so close to the surface. There was a lot of pain here to release. I knew I had her son with me. I had to get this right. I took a step back in my head and described what I had seen and experienced: "I am holding a steering wheel and it is going all over the place. All I can see is white. I can't control it."

"That's exactly right," said his mum. I could see she was relieved that I really did have her son with me but I was perplexed. There was a steering wheel, yet he wasn't in a car?

Mum lost no time in explaining. "My son was in a plane. He was delivering aid in Africa when the plane was shot down."

The audience was stunned as Mum relayed the details of her son's passing. I have never experienced such an attentive audience and I could sense that everyone felt for this lady and her young daughter. It was clear that having him communicate with them, although causing tears, was helping enormously. They really needed to know that he was truly alright and were so pleased to have him come through. At last they would be able to find some peace.

How awful to have a son who was such a beautiful soul, so loving and giving and have him die like that in his prime, when he was doing something so worthwhile. I don't think anyone in the audience will forget this story of the brave young soul who gave his life for others. It put everything else into perspective. I know it is a story I hold dear to my heart, that such incredible souls walk amongst us and had it not been for the show we would not have known of his bravery. He deserved to be talked about. The family deserved to have the good work he did acknowledged. Sometimes, often, it just seems so unfair – why do the good die young? And just what can you say to people who have loved and lost such souls? All I can do is let them know that they are alright and hope and pray that somehow, some way, they will give me the right words to say. Here was a good man. Losing him hurt, more than I have hurt this lifetime. There were no 'right' words. The comfort came not from words but from knowing that he did live on, because both Mum and sister knew that there was no way that I could have known the circumstances of his passing. Circumstances I so very nearly got 'wrong'.

This experience heightened my awareness of the dangers of trying to interpret the information given. The stakes can be high when the need to receive a message is so great. The pressures of giving the necessary proof can be similarly high and if I interpret the information wrongly I can make mistakes as I initially did here. Of course with hindsight it was easy to work out. The steering wheel was a plane steering wheel, the white – what I thought was ice – was clouds, and the skidding feeling was how it felt to lose control of a plane. I have never flown a plane, let alone lost control of one and so I didn't recognise how it felt when it came through. The nearest thing I could think of was a car in a skid. Thankfully, I had the presence of mind to back-track and describe what I was seeing and experiencing. It was an experience that reminded me just how important it can be at times not to interpret the information I am given but just to describe what I am seeing, hearing or experiencing and let the loved ones here make sense of it. They can and often do make a far better job of it than I.

Laughter is the Best Medicine

We knew we were in for a good night when very early on in a show one gentleman spirit, the late husband of a lady in the audience, decided to try and get into my body with me. At first, I did not know what was happening. I was standing in the aisle looking at a lady in the audience when all of a sudden I felt a male spirit trying to get into my body. Usually spirits come in on my left-hand side and they move their consciousness into mine gently, until they are partly in me and partly out of me. Then they communicate with me in words, pictures and feelings. This one was different, very different. I didn't yet know who he was and there were no 'part in, part out' niceties. He wanted to get inside me, completely! I asked internally if he was linked with the lady I was looking at and he said, "Yes, she is my wife." Again I felt him. He was coming into my body and that's all there was to it. I called out silently for my guides to help but seemingly nothing happened. He was huge, really huge.

My facial expressions must have shown my surprise and consternation because the audience was laughing spontaneously at me and I wasn't even speaking. I was totally focused on coping with what was happening to me, so much so that I had not even been able to share with the audience what was going on. What was he doing? I took a few steps forward and then a few steps back to balance myself. I must have looked like a drunken person not able to coordinate what I was doing. I held onto the back of the nearest chair to steady myself. What was he trying to do? Had he not communicated through a medium before? He didn't need to be this forceful; mediumship is a graceful art. "I am a delicate instrument," I tried to tell him in my head. It made no difference, he wasn't listening to me and instead kept coming in to me. "Where on earth were my guides?" I asked internally for help to manage this one, but no one seemed to want to help. I was still totally focused on what was happening to me; it was as if the audience did not exist. I realised that several minutes had gone by since I had interacted with the audience and I looked up to see how they were responding to what was happening to me. Judging by their facial expressions they were enjoying watching the experience unfold. It was like trying to squeeze a genie back into a bottle and I was the all-too-small bottle. I was getting very hot and feeling rather like a large Michelin Man. I felt big inside my skin but I knew I didn't look any different. This loved one was clearly determined to get through.

Suddenly, it dawned on me. This might be his way of giving me a message and surely this must have something to do with size. Perhaps *his* size. "Was your husband a really big man?" I asked when after a few moments I could finally speak. The response confirmed my thoughts. "Six foot seven," his wife said. He felt every inch of that to me! I am five foot four so you can imagine it was a tight squeeze. The audience found it hilarious. Even though I hadn't said anything prior to this, they could see that something was going on with my body and this simple exchange clarified for them what had been happening. We all enjoyed the joke. The gentleman had found a really humorous way to put across his size, which was his key distinguishing feature – perfect proof that it was indeed him. There are not that many men in New Zealand who are six feet seven inches tall.

No sooner had he got across his size than he was laughing about his teeth. Raucous, booming laughter was vibrating through me and there was a strong smell of alcohol. This man was 'larger than life' in more than just his size! "Why is he laughing about his teeth?" I managed to ask when I could keep from laughing myself. His wife laughed too and explained the story.

He had got really drunk one night, lost his false teeth down the toilet and had to fish them out. It had not been pretty. There was no doubt about it. This spirit was definitely the lady's husband. Tears of laughter were rolling down the wife's face and her son next to her was laughing too. The whole audience was enjoying this message. I had asked for some laughter to lighten the evening and I certainly got it. No wonder my guides had not intervened. They knew what was happening and that there wasn't cause for concern, quite the opposite in fact. It was a way of getting a really strong message across, which in itself gave wonderful proof. He left effortlessly, once he had got his own way, and the feeling of my body returned to normal.

It never ceases to amaze me just how fitting some of the evidence is that loved ones in spirit world provide. I always add in the extra requirement that the messages provide twice as much laughter as tears. Sometimes, the laughter is at my expense and sometimes it is just a humorous memory that those here share with their loved ones, as the six-foot-seven husband's had been. The laughter helps keep the shows from getting too emotional and helps audiences leave feeling inspired rather than emotionally drained.

When a relative has passed over recently and thinking about them is still emotional for those I speak to, I ask specifically for something to lighten the situation. The following interlude with Graham and his wife is a lovely example of the kind of information that can come through.

Graham had passed quickly and recently, so once I had confirmed with his wife that it was her husband that I had with me, she and her two daughters-in-law joined me on stage. I could see the emotion was still raw for all three so asked for some humour to help them cope. Immediately, I saw the top corner of a made bed, the place where you would usually put a pillow.

"Graham is showing me the top right-hand corner of a bed, a made bed – do you know why he would be doing that?"

The lady on stage with me smiled. "Yes, I know what he means. That will be our bed," she said.

Now spirits do not just show me beds for no reason – I mean everyone has a bed. There had to be something significant about the bed.

"Why is he showing me your bed? What is significant about it?" I asked curiously, sensing that there was something humorous in store but for the life of me I couldn't imagine what that might be. I've heard just about every weird and unusual thing from spirit world and people here during shows but her response took even me by surprise.

"It's where I keep his ashes," came her response.

The audience erupted into laughter. No one had

expected that response. "Does anyone else keep the ashes of their loved ones on their bed?" I checked with the audience to make sure it wasn't just me thinking that was unusual. From the continued laughter that ensued, apparently not.

The lady was giggling away herself, enjoying the humour as much as everyone else.

"Your husband is shaking his head," I continued. I wasn't sure what he meant. "He's pointing to the bed again. I think he's worried about the ashes being there."

"Do you know, I often worry about them too," she went on, obviously much more relaxed now. "The grandchildren sit on our bed to watch TV and I am worried that one of these days they will have a pillow fight and my husband will be all over the bedroom."

Well that was it! I could barely speak, the audience was in fits and many people had tears running down their faces. But there was more to come. "In fact," she said, "I worry about what I will do if it ever does happen – I'd have to vacuum him up!" It took a while for us all to get over the hilarious picture that all this conjured up. This time we needed the tissues for the tears of laughter that were rolling down our cheeks but eventually some form of order was restored. The humour had relaxed his wife and Graham was then able to send a more serious message to his wife and daughters-in-law. He told them how much he loved them all and let the girls know that he had always looked on them as his daughters – they had always felt that close and special to him.

How very wonderful is the humour that spirit world graces us with at times; sometimes just to lighten our hearts and at other times providing an atmosphere that enables another more serious or significant message to be conveyed.

Getting the Message Across

Creating a successful show is determined by many factors: my own energy levels and openness, the mood and receptivity of the audience and Andrew's ability to ensure any unwanted spirits are not allowed to interfere. There are also practical considerations such as the audience's comfort, the size and shape of the room, the temperature and the sound quality. Last, but by no means least, is the ability of loved ones in spirit world to get their messages through. The 'larger than life' story in the previous chapter is an example of a spirit with no problem in this area. Some spirits are more skilled at communicating than others and some have not had much practice before. In the same way that some people make better mediums, some spirits are better communicators from the other side – just as some people are good Pictionary players and others aren't! So how do loved ones in spirit world communicate with us? Mainly spirits use telepathy and this is made up of a mix of the traditional symbols and the 'new' way: a mix of images, words, feelings and concepts or knowings. They use all the traditional five senses, seeing, hearing, touching, tasting and smelling and an inner sixth sense of knowing.

Imagine that you had to use telepathy to send a sunset to a friend. How could you best send it? Could you hold the complete image in your mind and then use your will to project it to them? Would you write down the word 'sunset' and project that, or would you hold the concept of warmth and the movement of the sun setting? Or would you do something else entirely? These are the choices that they have to make in the spirit world side. Projecting the information takes mental discipline and will-power, qualities that hopefully we acquire while we are in physical life. Spiritual loved ones are also able, using the assistance of my guides, to access my memory banks. So for example, if they want to pass on the name 'Karen' the easiest way is to show me an image of my sister Karen from my memory banks.

It isn't always that simple though. An image of my sister may be shown to me for other reasons than just her name. It could be used to show a sister link or it could be used, at present, to show that someone is pregnant, as my sister is expecting a baby at the moment. The spirit may look like my sister or the spirit may have similar personality traits to my sister. The only way you can find out what is meant is through practice. Lots and lots of practice, so that you can develop a whole range of symbols and meanings with your guides. The more mediumship I do the more my guides are able to refine the way we work together and improve the quality of the survival evidence; the evidence of life after death, that we are able to provide.

Both Spirit and I are learning through my experiences. Some spirits have more to learn than others. For example, a spirit that has only recently passed over may need the assistance of a spirit who has been passed over for longer. This is evidenced by grandparents often coming through first to help set up the link, and then bringing through other family members. Sometimes I see them clearly and sometimes I simply sense their energy, age and gender. The nearest way I can think to describe how it feels is this: imagine being in a room with your eyes closed. Someone comes in and using your inner senses you sense whether they are male or female, young or old, family or a friend. Some spiritual energies are clear and easy to sense and others less so.

Where I see spirits standing in relation to the living person is also significant. As I look at a living person, their father and his family stand to their immediate right and their mother and her family to their immediate left. Dad's parents then appear behind him and Mum's behind her. Children and recent passings appear in front of the person and partners, friends and siblings alongside. Cousins and nephews are shown to me with a diagonal link. So the whole picture looks very much like a living family tree. Second marriages, adoptions and half-brothers and sisters can be harder to discern. Usually I have to ask questions internally to make sure of their relationship to the person I am talking to. Basically I am open to receive information in whatever form it comes. If I don't understand an image I say internally 'show me in a different way', or 'tell me' and if I don't understand a concept or idea 'please explain differently'. Sometimes it can take a while but usually, if I stay with it long enough, I can make sense of what spirits mean. During the shows I take the stronger, easier links from Spirit as people do not want to see me sitting silently for most of the show trying to understand what the messages that are given mean.

In addition to the images, words and concepts there are other subtle ways that our loved ones can let us know that it is really them, and that is through the choice of words and manner of speaking that they inspire in me. Often a phrase will come out of my mouth that I personally would not use, or my way of speaking may become more abrupt or the tone or pitch of my voice may be similar to the way the loved one in spirit used to speak. Many people have commented on it over the years and as the following story illustrates, David's father was a spirit who used this particular method.

David was a middle-aged man who was sitting quite close to the front of the audience. I could feel his deceased father's presence with him very strongly.

"Has your father passed over?" I enquired, to make sure I was with the right person.

"Yes, he has," replied David.

"And was it a very sudden passing that took everyone by surprise?"

"Yes it was," he said looking down. "Would you like to come up on stage with me?" I gently enquired. He agreed but I could tell he was a little apprehensive about joining me on stage.

His dad came through more strongly as we sat on the stage together.

"Your dad is showing me that you were very close when he died but not actually with him. It almost feels like you were in the next room."

"Not quite," he said "but I know what he means. He was inside the house and I was outside."

Suddenly, my heart started to pound and I found my right hand holding my heart. This could only mean one thing. "He's showing me that he had a massive heart attack," I managed.

I was thankful that this had been shown clearly to me without manifesting itself as a real heart attack. When I was less experienced, I had once held a chain belonging to the son of a man who had died suddenly of a massive heart attack. The father's spirit came in so strongly and forcefully that I almost experienced a heart attack myself. Another person had to literally prise the chain out of my fingers as my hand was clenched so tightly. As the chain was released from my grip, so too the symptoms of a heart attack receded. It was an experience I will never forget and one which I learned from. Now I ensure I am connected at the right level so any attack is not too strong and I can control the experience better.

The audience was anxious to hear his response to my description of the father's passing. The man on stage was a younger man and it would not be expected that he would have lost his father. "That's right," said his son. "Dad died very suddenly from a massive heart attack." He was obviously impressed with the information and so was the audience.

When I next spoke I noticed that my voice didn't sound like my normal voice, it was deeper and coarser, but still very much my voice.

"Dad's smiling about the wedding," I said. "Boy you took your time!" Dad teased, speaking through me. The son grinned; he had dated his fiancée for some 14 years. "We got married after he died," the son confirmed.

Dad also showed me that he liked the 'girl' his son had married. David had known that his dad had approved of his partner before he died but was glad Dad had affirmed this again.

I worked hard with the father to bring through information that would give further proof but not upset the son too much in front of everyone. Dad had come through because the sudden nature of his passing meant that there was no time for him to say goodbye to his son or to other family members and he wanted them to be at peace. It's funny; we want them to be at peace and they want us to be at peace. We *all* can be if we open up the lines of communication between the dimensions. He knew that his son felt guilty that he had been outside when he had had the heart attack. David often blamed himself for not being inside at that moment so he could have helped and he worried that his dad may have called out and he did not hear him.

David's dad explained, through me, that he was not a man who could express his feelings very well while here, and even on the other side he found it hard to say what he wanted to say. He wanted David to know that there was nothing he could have done even if he had been inside; the heart attack had been too severe. He wanted him to know he loved him and he should feel no guilt. I forget the precise words that came through, perhaps because they were words that I would not normally say myself, but I do remember that David completely understood what was said and said that even some of the words I used to express his dad's thoughts were exactly the ones his dad would have used when he was alive. So often our loved ones are just like we remember them; their choice of words, their sense of humour and sometimes even their way of speaking seems to find its way out of my mouth. It is another way loved ones in spirit world can let you know it really is them. It's another proof, if you like.

Over the years I have been shown that passing on messages such as this, whether they be the absolution of guilt, reconciliation or expressions of love not communicated while here, have benefits for both the people here and the departed souls. Here we get to heal past hurts that we may not even have been fully conscious of; sometimes we are angry that they have left us. Spirit world side, they get the chance to put something right, find their peace, and so move on with their own spiritual journeys.

I find that when I work as a medium I am receiving information on many different levels all at once. I may be paying attention to what I am seeing internally and listening to the words, when I notice that a part of my body has assumed an unusual position or I no longer have use of it or it hurts. At one show my legs went from beneath me as soon as I tried to link with a particular lady. I propped myself up on the chair at the end of the aisle with my elbows while I continued to talk to her. I disappeared out of sight of most of the audience and momentarily worried that the audience must have wondered what on earth was going on. I reassured myself that they would still be able to hear my voice and continued. You see, to me it is not that strange to suddenly lose the use of a part of my body. It happened to me a lot when I was healing regularly in the past and now manifests itself as a way of getting a message across. I am quite used to it now and of course I know nothing happens without a reason. My guides protect me well and so usually losing control of a part of my body is a sign of a strong link with someone who has passed over and the body part affected is usually significant in some way. In this case my legs were completely useless to me and although it must have looked pretty odd, I continued with the link.

"I can see your grandmother on your mother's side," I explained.

"Yes, she passed a little while ago. We were very close," came the response. I could see there was a strong link between the grandmother and the lady in the audience, because as we spoke the grandmother moved really close to her beloved granddaughter. I couldn't wait to ask about the legs.

"Did your grandmother have something wrong with her legs?" I asked, pointing down to mine. The audience laughed. Now they realised what was happening.

"Yes, she was in a wheelchair for much of her life as she was completely paralysed," she said smiling. She too had realised the significance of my strange behaviour.

Of course, that was exactly what I was experiencing, a paralysis of my legs. As soon as we 'understood that message' the use of my legs came back to me and I could stand again to deliver the rest of the message. It was quite a relief. Her grandmother was very pleased with herself, at how well she had communicated. The granddaughter certainly had no doubt who it was. Her grandmother was able to communicate that now she could move wherever she wanted at will and she was with Grandad, who had died some years previously. She was a very determined lady with an extreme way of giving proof to her granddaughter.

This range of examples of messages from shows illustrates the many ways I get messages from Spirit that together enable me to give accurate information. I often wonder what the spirits and my guides will think of next – they certainly know how to keep me on my toes and will stop at nothing to get their messages through.

There are many, many spirits wanting to communicate with us and not nearly enough mediums to do this kind of work. Part of my role over the coming years is to be something of an ambassador for the spiritual dimensions and raise the respectability of the profession, so that more people are motivated to do what I do and people are not afraid to develop what are, after all, natural abilities. It is not a responsibility I take lightly. Even now I am still learning how to perfect what I do to take my mediumship to the next level and to understand how to communicate more clearly and more effectively. It's funny; when I first started communicating with spirit world my aim was to get messages as clear as they are on the phone. Now I realise just how limiting a goal that was. Communication with spirits can be clearer than it is face-to-face, let alone on the telephone. Telepathy can give us a complete knowing of the loved one in spirit world if we allow it to. It can be an incredibly beautiful experience and is the kind of new mediumship style I continuously seek to develop further.

What Happens When We Die?

One of the questions I am asked most frequently at the shows is understandably, "What happens when we die?"

I guess I will know for sure when I pass over myself, but for now the best understanding I have is that no one passes over alone. There is always at least one loved one that comes for them.

Diana was a beautiful lady who was terminally ill with lung cancer. Her daughter Lisa had contacted me to see if I could help her mother with healing and general support. The cancer had spread widely and in her late 70s, Diana was feeling that she did not want to fight, she no longer had the energy for it. The healing sessions revolved around lessening the pain and helping Diana feel more peaceful with the prospect of dying. As Diana's condition deteriorated, she became less and less coherent and morphine was causing her to drift in and out of consciousness.

"She's been talking about her brother Tom again," Diana's daughter Lisa said, as I arrived for the half-weekly healing session. "She says he's standing in the corner of the room, but I can't see anything. Do you think it is just the morphine?"

"No, I don't. I think she is *really* seeing him." I knew Lisa hadn't really accepted that her mum was dying. She was clinging on to any glimmer of hope, however remote.

I knew I had to begin to explain what was to come but I also knew that my explanation, no matter how kindly put, would start to break the daughter's fragile world.

"When we get near the end we start to be able to see into the other dimensions to the people that are waiting there for us. Your mum's brother is waiting for her so that she doesn't pass on her own. He will take her through to where she needs to go," I said gently.

"Are you saying my mum is going to die?" the daughter asked. I knew the doctors and nurses had already told her this but somehow it hadn't sunk in. Mum was fading fast now, and her daughter just didn't want to accept it.

How I would have loved to be anywhere but in that room at that time. The silence was almost unbearable as I sought frantically for the 'right' way to respond. An internal debate raged. Over the years I've seen older people not being told how sick they were and not being able to say their goodbyes until it was too late, and situations where some relatives knew what was going on and some didn't. I've wondered how the ones who knew that their loved one was dying coped with the knowledge. It must have been a huge burden for them to bear – knowing but pretending that everything was alright. More recently, working as a healer I have seen people deteriorate alarmingly quickly as soon as they are diagnosed with cancer – many effectively have given up hope once the 'Big C' was diagnosed. Prognosis is the doctor's domain rather than mine, but so often the doctors tell terminally ill patients what they don't want to hear and so they are often desperate to seek out anyone who will tell them something different, tell them that everything will be alright.

I had learned through experience that my attitude to events and situations shapes them to a certain extent. If I expect to meet inconsiderate drivers on the road I probably will; if I expect to meet courteous drivers I probably will. Did it follow then that if I expect to get better I probably will and if I expect to die I probably will? I didn't yet understand to what extent our attitude or expectations shaped events but I did recognise that there was a link. How should I answer Lisa's question? All physical signs were that Mum was deteriorating. I didn't want, though, to be responsible for the daughter losing hope and starting to think negatively about Mum's condition – that wouldn't help anyone, least of all Mum, but I didn't want to give false hope either.

I took a deep breath and asked for guidance in finding the 'right' words to help Lisa. Thankfully, they came.

"All I can say is that the phenomenon you describe, your mum seeing her brother in the room, sounds like what I have heard happening when people get ready to make the transition. They start to develop the ability to see into the next dimension in readiness for their transition. That way, it isn't so much of a shock to their system. It isn't for me to say whether she will live or die but I can see she has deteriorated over the past few weeks. What has the doctor said?"

"He is always so negative. He has been from the start. You are the only one who has been positive," Lisa said.

Again I thought hard about my reply. "All I do is focus on what the situation is *now* – because that is all we are able to deal with. Our mind can race ahead into the future and think about what may or may not happen, but when it does that we are no longer present here and now. Here and now there may be things you can do to make Mum more comfortable or to ease her pain. There may be things you can do to lift her spirits and put a smile on her face. But when you are thinking about the future, you are not fully present and you may miss the small things you could be doing right now to help her. Everything we do here and now makes a difference. Concentrate on being here and now – doing what you can for Mum with the symptoms she has." It seemed to help. At least, Lisa did not press me again about whether her Mum was going to die.

Diana was moved into the local hospice about a week later and passed away peacefully during the following week. Diana's daughter went into shock; she really did not want to believe that her mum had died. I saw her at the funeral, her posture stiff with grief as she made her way through the other mourners.

"How are you doing?" I asked when we got the chance to speak to each other.

"Not good," she said. "I didn't want her to die."

"I know," I said holding her hand. I could feel the depth of her pain. She had truly loved her mother.

"I saw Mum in a dream last night," she said looking down. "She showed me she was alright now and with Tom, her brother."

I nodded silently that I understood.

"I didn't see her for very long," she paused to collect herself. "It was so real." The daughter's eyes were misting as she remembered the dream. I could see that she was trying desperately not to break down in front of people.

"It *was* real," I said. "She was showing you that she was alright and that the pain had gone."

The daughter looked up at me searchingly as I explained carefully: "Lots of people dream about their loved ones after they have passed. It is often their way of letting us know that they are alright and that they are safely through to the next dimension. She is in a better place now. You will be able to see her again in your dreams if you want to and she will be able to reassure you that she really is alright."

"Do you know, I have felt better since I had the dream?" Lisa said, wiping a tear from her eye. "I just loved her so much." The daughter's voice trailed off and instinctively we hugged.

"I know," I said softly. "Don't ever stop loving her." And then after a few moments, "She can still feel your love. Remember to keep loving her and remember that loving her doesn't hurt; it's your thought that she is not still here that is causing you the pain. And if I know your mum, I am sure she will find lots of ways in the days ahead of letting you know she is still here."

I have found that the phenomenon of seeing the spirit of loved ones who have already passed over before we die, as Diana did, is remarkably common. It is also common for people who have had near-death experiences to describe it as seeing a white tunnel. Even very young children who could not possibly have heard other people's descriptions of near-death experiences have described the experience as a tunnel so it seems reasonable to assume that this is what we will experience.

What does this mean? Why do we see loved ones who have passed over and why do we see a white tunnel? My understanding is that it appears to be a tunnel because on death we move through into a lighter dimension. It is lighter in terms of frequency (love) and lighter in terms of light (truth). In this lighter dimension, the higher part of ourselves awaits us to remind us of who we truly are. When the physical body is about to die our 'higher aspect' pulls our spirit back from the physical body and as it does so we leave many of our fears and limiting beliefs (our darkness) behind.

It is my understanding that when we die we leave our flesh-and-blood body behind and only take with us into this lighter dimension our seven vibrating energy bodies. These vibrating energy bodies can be felt or sensed by most people. Seeing them, however, takes more practice. The density of the seven energy bodies decreases the further away from the physical body they are. The first and densest energy body is just a few centimetres away from the body, the next, a bit further out and so on. It looks similar to a Russian doll with each successive energy body enclosing and filling the last. The seventh energy body can extend several metres from the physical body and is much finer in vibration and harder to sense.

For each energy body there is a corresponding 'heaven' or dimension. The lower three dimensions are denser and more fear based and commonly referred to as the astrals. The four higher heavens are love based. When I work in public as a medium I only work with the loving dimensions. If a soul is capable of feeling love it will go to one of these higher dimensions when it passes; what most of us commonly think of as heaven.

For many of us, dreaming is the nearest thing to dying that we will experience before we actually pass over, as sometimes when we dream we take these energy bodies with us and experience different dimensions or realities. If you have ever felt yourself 'jolt' back into your body when sleeping you have 'travelled' to these dimensions. Some people call it astral travelling and describe a silver cord that attaches the energy bodies to the physical body. When we die the sensation is like dreaming but there is no cord to pull us back into our physical body.

If someone passes peacefully in their sleep, it may be that the experience of dying is like having a dream from which they do not awaken.

When someone passes suddenly the spirit leaves the body very quickly and almost goes into shock, experiencing itself as separate to the physical body, which it now sees as an empty shell. Frequently this shock is followed by an immediate thought of someone close to them who is still living and who needs to know that they are alright. If the intent is clear and focused the spirit then goes straight to that person. For me, this explains why so many people 'know' that a loved one has died before the news comes.

Loved ones in spirit are usually around to help the person passing come to terms with what is happening to them; that they have no physical body but nevertheless still 'exist'. Without a physical body to direct, the spirit moves through time and space effortlessly and at will. They often need the assistance of a more experienced spirit when they first pass over, to guide them in how to travel in their new body and to answer the many questions about what has happened and how life is on the other side. Where there has been severe damage to the physical body through massive injury the energy bodies of the spirit need healing and repair. Then it appears that they go into a dimension to adjust and recuperate before moving on to the dimension that they are entitled to. People with long, drawn out, terminal illnesses that really ravaged their physical bodies, such as cancer, also tend to go to this place. The disease (dis-ease; when we are not at 'ease' with ourselves energy gets blocked and if not treated will cause disease) affects not only the physical form but also the energy bodies, particularly those energy bodies close to the physical body. With Diana, this recuperation phase would have been very necessary and that is why her brother Tom came through in the way that he did to assist her with her transition. By herself she may not have had the energy to move through to spirit world properly and could have become earth bound.

How long the spirit spends in such a place of healing is determined entirely by individual circumstances. Diana had to rest there while her energy bodies healed sufficiently to hold the higher frequency of energy that she would need to move through into the dimension or heaven that she was entitled to go to. The appropriate dimension, or heaven, is determined by the spiritual progress the individual has made throughout their lifetimes, not just this one. I have known quite 'difficult' people to be in a much higher kingdom/heaven than anyone would have given them credit for, which sometimes makes me wonder if 'difficult' people aren't sometimes simply playing roles to teach others here what they most need to learn. Another reason why we should not judge one another! Perhaps the most intolerable person in your life is your greatest teacher!

I saw Diana briefly some months later and she showed me she was in one of the higher dimensions with loved ones all around. She had moved through successfully and was very excited about all her experiences. Diana continued to try to communicate with her daughter through her dreams but I know there were frustrations on both sides. Both wanted communication clearer than it was. It seems we cannot receive any more than we are ready to receive and no amount of effort or will-power can allow knowledge through, unless the recipient is truly open to it. Diana's daughter did remember seeing her mum but not much more than that, so perhaps her limiting beliefs were affecting their communication. In the past, I did not know that higher dimensions existed and even when I became aware, I can remember how my own limiting beliefs affected my interpretation of the kingdoms or dimensions and how life was there. Since then my awareness has expanded but perhaps even now I am not seeing the full picture. I suspect there is much more to it than I have experienced and I recognise that my learning and understanding of the different dimensions is not yet complete.

Diana's fondest wish spirit world side was that she had known that there was nothing to fear about death before she died. Then perhaps her daughter would not have been so afraid of her dying. In my mind I was reminded of how many years ago in some ancient cultures there was the ability to die consciously, to say

84

your goodbyes to family and friends and go to a special place and just let go. The feeling of dying seems not to be that much different to how we feel when we let ourselves go to sleep, except instead of dreaming we awaken. We awaken from the dream of this existence and who we think we are, to who we *truly* are. It is more incredible and more wonderful than we ever imagined.

Children

Of all the messages I receive, those I receive from children are the hardest for me to bear and trigger the most tears. I know the children are alright, in a better place, but I also recognise that I do not and cannot fully appreciate all that the family has been through and the pain they are feeling.

I know that there is no death. I have known this now for over 10 years. I know that what we call death is simply a transformation from one form into another. In much the same way as a caterpillar changes into a butterfly, we leave our physical form behind and take on our spiritual form. Knowing this doesn't make passing on the messages from children any easier. I know that their loved ones here still feel the pain of missing them – often intensely. As I connect with the loved ones here to bring through messages for them, I feel the strength of their feelings very briefly. It often leaves me stunned at how much pain some people are living with day in and day out. I have not known such pain in this lifetime and I often feel at a loss for words and an unworthy bearer of the message.

I have learned the hard way that how I pass on a message from a child has to be handled with the utmost care and sensitivity. In a way, I have to almost forget what I know about there being no death to even start to understand how the ones left behind feel, and to appreciate what they have been through. It doesn't get any easier, but as painful as it is at times, the feedback I have received from parents shows me how beneficial such communications are. Yes, there are tears, but often they are tears of joy and healing. Often there is healing in moments that in therapy would take years. The lovely stories that follow from Simon and Amy illustrate this beautifully.

I felt a small hand in mine as I stood close to a smartly dressed woman at the start of one of the shows. "She's there," he whispered excitedly to me. It felt as though he was whispering right in my ear. I could feel his soft breath on my cheek, which I knew wasn't physically possible, but I could sense it nevertheless. I could feel him holding my hand at the same time as he was whispering in my ear, which should have made him adult sized, but instead I knew that he wasn't that tall, perhaps just two years old. I also knew that his knowledge was way beyond that of a two-year-old and that despite his tender age he would be able to communicate clearly because his intent was both strong and clear.

When I saw him, the sight of him quite took my breath away. I saw him in my mind's eye, full sized – he was an absolute sweetheart. A shock of ruffled blonde hair framed an angelic looking face. He had been a good child, full of love and good humour. I could sense his happy disposition. I knew that he was sorely missed. In seconds, the image of him disappeared and I could feel him back inside me again, trying to communicate.

Usually when children come through, a parent or a grandparent makes a link with me first and then helps the more recently passed soul communicate. As far as I know, this is because they have been in spirit world longer and are more familiar with how things work. They know, for example, how to direct their will and convey information telepathically to a medium such as myself. I believe that they can also help hold the frequencies at the required level for effective communication by radiating love and peace and that this plays a significant part in helping the newer members of spirit world come through. In this instance though, a parent or grandparent had not made contact first and this initially took me by surprise. I didn't yet understand why this should be but didn't have time to dwell on it as my attention was focused keenly on the lady the young boy was directing me to. She had long dark hair tied back from her face. Her complexion was pale and I could see visible tension lines around her mouth. Her eyes were sad, yet hopeful; they looked as though they had shed many tears. She looked away as I looked towards her, almost as though she dare not hope for a message. I knew it would be too much to tell her that I had her much-loved son with me straight away so I decided I'd find someone else to bring through for her first. I bought myself some time by walking up and down the aisle near where she sat until I eventually managed to link with the lady's grandmother on her mother's side in spirit world. I do not summon the spirit – rather, I put out a heartfelt plea for a loved one who has been in spirit world longer to come forward to help me with the link. Her maternal grandmother had come forward in response to my request, so that was where I would start. Despite his physical years, the young boy with me understood the need to go slowly; he was an old soul, but only on this earth in his most recent life for a very brief time. I wondered whether his being an old soul and having many previous incarnations and thus many previous times in spirit world was making it easier for him to link with me by himself.

I moved back to stand in front of the lady and this time she looked straight back at me. For a split second she had perhaps feared not getting a message, more than she feared receiving one. Now she was ready.

"I have your grandmother on your mother's side with you," I said, closely noticing the lady's reaction. I had to gauge how safe it was to talk about her son. I knew he had not been passed that long, as I could sense that there was still an enormous amount of emotion around her. It also felt like he was her only son.

The lady said yes, her grandmother had passed over. "Helen," I heard and immediately passed the name on. "She is giving me the name Helen."

"Ellen was my grandmother's name," she quickly affirmed.

"Ellen *is* your grandmother's name," Ellen in spirit world retorted equally quickly through me. The lady in the audience smiled. "Yes, that would be my grandmother. She believed fully in an afterlife. She always said she would still be here after she died and she's obviously still as adamant now as she was before!"

"She has a little boy with her," I began. The lady's smile vanished as her mouth tightened to a line. "He is alright. Your grandmother is looking after him for you." I knew I couldn't take this lady on stage. It would be too emotional and I felt the whole audience was sensitive to this too. You could have heard a pin drop as I bent down to talk with her on her level.

"Is he alright?" the lady asked, her voice barely audible.

He seemed very happy to me, but I asked internally to ensure he was. "Very happy and tell Mummy I like the dog," I relayed without hesitation. In my mind's eye I could see him racing around with a puppy. I knew it was a girl dog but couldn't tell the breed, most likely a crossbreed.

"He knows about the dog?" Her surprise at this information was obvious.

How could I know that they had just got a dog? How could her son know about the dog? They had got the dog after he had died. Her face was a picture and I could see that she was slowly processing the implication of her son's message. "We have only just got her!" she exclaimed with tears in her eyes, slowly shaking her head in disbelief. You could see a dawning realisation sweeping her face. Not only was her son alright, alive and well in the spiritual side of life, but he was with her, with her as she went on with her life. Her face broke into a smile and I wondered if this was the first time she had really smiled since she had lost him.

"He was an old soul," I explained. It wasn't proof but she knew exactly what I meant. That was how her mother described him too.

At the end of the show there were more tears for both of us as Mum came to tell me more about her son.

As I suspected, she confirmed that he had been their only child. His name was Simon and he had died just before his second birthday. He passed peacefully in his sleep. At first they, the parents and the doctors, didn't know what had caused the death and so there had been a long drawn out investigation. It seemed that for some reason he just stopped breathing. There had been so many questions; not just the question of how he had died but, why? Why him? Why now? Why *their* son? What if he had been in their bed? What if they had looked in on him during the night? The questions had been endless and the nights sleepless. There had been no real answers and there had been no peace.

Because of the nature of the message, Mum now felt safe to confide that she had often sensed her son around her but had put it down to wishful thinking. She hadn't dared tell anyone, not even her husband. Now she knew this sensation was for real and her happiness at this realisation was enormous. The message, although brief, had meant so much to her. I found out subsequently that when she talked to her husband about the show and the message she received, he too had felt their son around, but hadn't wanted to say anything either. The son's message had got them talking about their feelings, which in turn had brought Mum and Dad closer together. So much so that they had decided to try for another baby.

Simon's message had triggered profound healing. Knowing their son was with them in spirit allowed them to heal the hurt they were feeling and reconnect with their feelings for him and for each other. They could reflect back on their time together as a family with happiness rather than pain and recognised truly for the first time that it was their fear of losing another child that was keeping them from being a family again. They chose not to let fear rule their lives, as they knew Simon would not have wanted that for them. They moved forward into their future knowing Simon was still with them and knowing that whatever the future had in store for them they would not let the fear of losing another child keep them from being a family once more. They had so much love to give.

The messages from children never cease to move both myself and the audience. They move us emotionally but they also cause something inside of us to shift. It is as though they cause us to journey with the bereaved into their life and into their pain, and then out the other side into the light of knowing that their loved ones really didn't die, and that if they didn't die, then our loved ones didn't die either. The pain of the bereaved is felt by us, albeit briefly, and then when their pain lifts so does our own. We can experience a roller-coaster of emotions but we always come out the other side.

The messages from children, although very different, are always profound.

Amy, a young girl in spirit of just three or four years, directed me to her mum in the audience.

"I have a young girl called Amy wanting to talk to you," I said, looking at an attractive woman in her early thirties. "She's standing just in front of you." Of course, the whole audience looked to see if they could see her too but when I 'see' I am using my inner vision. Where the spirit stands in relation to the living person is significant; 'in front of' indicates, for me, a child.

Before I could explain further, the lady had confirmed what I already knew, "My daughter's name was Amy."

Amy was busy showing me cells of her former physical body, as though through a microscope. She showed me the spheres of the cells, then the nucleus within the cells. She showed me the chromosomes within the nucleus and then the genes within the chromosomes. As she did so, I realised that she was trying to tell me that she had suffered from a genetic defect. The images disappeared simultaneously as I recognised I had correctly received her message. Amy also conveyed that this had been known since birth, by showing me herself as a baby.

I explained what I was receiving. "Amy is showing me her genes, that there was something wrong with them, a genetic defect and she is showing me that this was known from when she was born." Mum nodded.

"They always knew that they would not have long with me – but that didn't make the pain of losing me any less," she explained through me. I felt as though I was speaking with a child's voice, how I spoke when I was a child. Mum nodded, her eyes downcast. The lady next to her, a stranger, reached across to comfort her. We all felt for her and as hard as it was, I knew that I had to go on with the message.

"They had hoped I would prove the experts wrong but I didn't; I passed away more or less when they had been warned I would," Amy explained.

There was barely a dry eye in the house, including my own, as she told her mum, "Don't blame yourself. You didn't do anything wrong." Mum was in tears and I knew that enough had been said. They were healing tears. She was letting go of the blame she had put on herself and she was grieving for the daughter she had lost. She was letting go of the hurt she had unintentionally caused herself.

My thoughts and those of the audience were with her. How does one cope with something like that? Knowing that your child is going to die and that there is nothing you can do about it? That somehow it is because of the genes they have? I gave silent thanks that my own children were alive and well and felt many in the audience were doing the same. We couldn't bring Amy back but we could honour her memory and right then that meant being silent, turning inwards and feeling Mum's pain, sharing it with her, understanding what it must have been like for her – understanding what it is like to live with a death sentence on your young child, a death sentence you can do nothing about and then one morning waking up without them. Then the next morning and the next and the next. Not taking them to school. Not cooking their dinner. Not combing their hair. I have had my challenges this lifetime but nothing like that to deal with. I felt very humble and at a loss for what to say.

"She was a very special child," eventually came out of my mouth and yes, her Mum had felt that from day one.

I felt lost for words. It took a while before I was guided to continue the message and I chose not to fill the silence with talk. When Mum's tears had dried I felt Amy's spirit draw close once more. It was time to let her communicate again. Amy told me she had appeared to her mum frequently in dreams. Mum confirmed that she had dreamt about Amy on several occasions and each time the dreams had been really vivid but sort of unfinished. She didn't really understand what Amy was trying to tell her in the dreams.

Amy said she was having trouble getting through to her dad and that was what the dreams were about. She couldn't get through to her dad and so was trying doubly hard to get through to her mum. The support of the audience, which was predominantly women, gave Mum the strength to share.

"My husband is still finding it all very hard. He has just switched off."

"Don't give up on him Mum," came the heartfelt request from Amy in spirit world, "and I won't give up on him either."

Even in spirit world this beautiful soul was trying to help her Mum and Dad see the way forward, and encourage them to support each other and be positive about their future together. It was just what she did when she was here and it was just what Mum needed to hear. Tears rolled down Mum's face and it was clear that this was the moment I needed to let Amy go.

"I will leave you with Amy's love," I said as I slowly stepped back and gave Mum her space to feel Amy's love around her. Amy's love would always be with Mum and Dad, even if her dad couldn't feel it yet.

It was a moving communication with a simple but profound message that had brought most of the audience to tears. When we are in relationships, if we *really* want them to work, *we shouldn't give up on each other*.

Spirit world never, ever gives up on us. If you *really* love someone, you don't give up. It is spirit world's deep and abiding love for us that motivates them to communicate with us in whatever way they can, whenever they can. Age does not affect their ability to communicate with us, nor does any physical limitation they may have had while here. When they are determined to get through and the time is right they will stop at nothing to make their point and release you from your pain; release you from the illusion that they have died.

I asked myself, "Why do young souls such as Amy die? Why does there have to be so much pain and suffering? Why are these children taken from such loving families?"

There is a saying that 'only the good die young' and from my experience, I would have to say that I have met some incredibly beautiful souls who have sadly died at a young age. Is this saying true? If so, why? Internally I asked this question many times and finally got the following quiet response. The peacefulness of the reply contrasted so strongly with my own ardent questioning that it gave the words more significance than they already carried by themselves:

'Your question is perhaps based on a belief that death is a bad thing – what if it isn't?'

I guess the message or insight from my whole experience of working with children in spirit world is that from our limited emotional, intellectual and physical perspective we make a judgement as to whether an event is good or bad. My question 'why do the good die young?' was based on a perception that death *was* a bad thing. The teaching did not say that death was *not* a bad thing. Nor did it say that it was *not* a good thing. Death is as life is – neither good nor bad. The teaching showed me that we should not judge death. When we are judging something we are not fully embracing it. We are not 'in the moment' in life when we are in our heads judging it.

Also within my question 'why do the good die young?' was the implied belief that there are *good* and *bad* people and that it is possible to discern who is which. What constitutes a good person and a bad person? Who are we to judge? Much of the pain we experience from losing a loved one then stems from how we perceive things.

If a situation is painful to me, I now go within and ask from the depth of my being to be shown a different way of seeing or perceiving it. Sometimes I am shown a different way and sometimes I am not. However, I know beyond doubt that events that at first we consider dreadful, such as death, often have a way of turning into beautiful opportunities and help us to become more than we ever were before.

Perhaps when we lose a child this can be seen as their 'gift' to us. Their passing causes us and those around us considerable soul-searching. We start looking for answers with a fervency we have perhaps not experienced before. We cry out for help and we are relentless in our searching for answers. We cry out to know: Why? Why them? Why now? Why in this way? When we don't find the answers externally or in our heads, we start directing them internally to our heart. Perhaps the pain of losing a child or indeed any loved one physically from our lives is the pain of our heart centre opening more than ever before. Perhaps directing our questions internally allows us to connect more fully with our Soul allowing our spiritual connection with our loved one and with ourselves to open and expand. Perhaps in losing them we have an incredible opportunity to find ourselves and to be all that we can be.

It is difficult to find words to provide comfort or some form of reconciliation to those who have lost a child or indeed any loved one physically from their lives. I have other thoughts that explore this area more deeply, which I will articulate in further books, but at this stage my hope is that some of what I have expressed here will be a source of reflection and comfort for those who are struggling to come to terms with the death of a loved one.

A Lesson to Learn

Sometimes I am taken by surprise at the level of emotion a particular link in spirit world causes within me. I find the tears flowing uncontrollably as the loved one comes through and with some the tears flow even as I recount the story a long time afterwards. I know that each story that emerges during a show touches each person differently; some touch us more than others for different reasons.

In some cultures of the world crying is done openly and I believe that crying can be good for us. When we cry we are releasing something that we have been holding onto: thoughts, feelings, emotions or perhaps an old way of looking at the world or a situation. The more science-based view argues that tears allow us to release chemicals that build up during stressful times and releasing these chemicals is beneficial for our physical well-being. It seems to be considered by many that crying is indeed cathartic.

There are often tears at the shows. Sometimes it is the people on stage, sometimes it is the people observing in the audience and sometimes it is me. When the tears come, they come for a range of reasons. It may be our compassion for the person receiving the message, it may be our pain at losing one of our own loved ones or it may be past hurts or issues we are not even fully conscious of. Whichever it is, crying is a release – we are letting something go and in doing so healing a part of ourselves.

Michael's story I remember well because it touched me profoundly for reasons I did not fully understand at the time. Whenever I replayed his story in my head I would find tears rolling down my face. Midway through a show, Michael had stepped into my body almost without my knowing and walked me over to his mum who was sitting about halfway back in the audience. She was an attractive lady with a friendly open face. The bond between mother and son was strong; it felt as though he would always be a part of her. I guessed that Michael was about eight or nine from the way he interacted with me and I knew that this was going to be emotional, not only because he was her son but because he had 'been taken from her'. Michael was giving me the feeling that there was something very wrong not only with the way that he died but with what happened afterwards. I realised I would have to slow the flow of information down if I was going to make sense of it and not completely overwhelm his mum emotionally. I checked for any other loved ones in spirit world and didn't detect any older relatives – Michael was making this link by himself. He was very clear and had a childlike quality about him – a clarity and a simplicity that was endearing. He was doing this all by himself and was proud to be doing so.

"Have you lost a son?" I asked, crouching down and looking at the lady that had been pointed out to me. Mum nodded and said, "Yes, I have." I invited her on stage to receive a message as I knew the link with her son was already very strong. I wanted to make the most of the link while it was so clear and on the stage I could more easily keep other spirits at bay. As Mum got to her feet I recognised that she also knew this was going to be emotional but her need to receive the message overcame any anxieties about being in front of people.

No sooner were we seated than I found myself pedalling a pushbike. My physical legs were moving round and round and my arms were outstretched holding the handlebars. I was very grateful to be wearing trousers, had I been in a skirt the scene would have been even more entertaining for the front few rows than it already was. I was pedalling hard, veering to the right and then I was indicating with my right arm. It moved up and to the right to about waist height. Internally, it was as though I was transported; I was in the centre of the road waiting to turn right. As soon as I understood what was happening my consciousness was back in my body and I was on stage looking at Mum who had tears rolling down her face. The whole audience had seen the actions and had all worked out what I was doing themselves. I hardly had to say, "He is showing me he was on a pushbike and he was turning right." It was so obvious, it seemed superfluous, but I needed to know that this made sense to Mum. I knew what I was experiencing and I knew the audience could see what I was experiencing but did it make sense to Mum in terms of how her son had died?

Mum nodded and explained that he had been killed in a road accident and had been on his bike at the time. The audience gasped. I was right about it being a strong link.

"It wasn't my fault Mum," came the child's voice through me "It wasn't my fault." It felt as though every hair on my body was on end. "I was waiting to turn right."

Tears were rolling down my face. The feeling inside was that Michael had been blamed for the accident when he actually had done nothing wrong. He had done everything properly, the way he had been taught. His distress about being blamed for something he had not done was coming over strongly. He had been killed. He had not caused the accident.

"My son had Downs Syndrome," his mother took time to explain. "He was always very good on his bike. I didn't think he had been at fault." After the accident it had been implied that he had been in the wrong and that perhaps Mum shouldn't have let him cycle on the road. Michael wanted the record put straight and he did so decisively. In spirit world he was clear, a bright light, who was able to communicate as well as any other spirit I have encountered. Once his message was communicated, he was at peace and left as quickly and as unnoticeably as he entered. He had left behind a gift. He had given his mum peace. She now knew that her feelings about the 'accident' were confirmed. Her son had been a competent bike rider, the accident had not been his fault, neither he nor she were to blame. Even more importantly, her much loved son Michael lived on in spirit world. He lived.

It was after the show had ended that my tears really started to flow and took me by surprise. There had been many emotional messages during the evening. Why was it that this one upset me more than the others? I replayed the message in my head. The riding on the bike, the indication to turn right and Michael's indignation that the 'accident' had not been his fault. I realised that for me the tears were not just about the tragedy of his passing and the pain Mum was feeling. They were because I had not realised before how losing a child with Down's Syndrome is no less painful than losing another child. Somehow, unconsciously, I had valued children with a disability as being less than 'normal' children. Somehow, I had thought that losing them would not be as painful – perhaps it would even be a blessing. This belief buried deep in my unconsciousness had been brought into the bright light of Michael's and his mother's love for each other and I could see all too clearly how wrong I had been. The love between Michael and his Mum was as strong as any I have experienced and I felt deep shame. Somehow, somewhere along my path I had bought into the idea that disabled people are somehow less than the rest of us and this deep realisation brings tears to my eyes even now.

Every one of us is equally important. We may not have apparent equality in the circumstances of our lives or in our abilities but nevertheless, we are all equally important and equally deserving of love. The tears I cried that night were for me, for my lack of understanding, for my ignorance.

The Right Space and Place

At one venue I had my first experience of someone who hadn't been able to get a ticket to the show refusing to leave reception and making the hotel staff feel really uncomfortable. The lady was very upset. I did not know what was going on until the duty manager came to see me. He explained that the lady had only decided to buy a ticket a few hours before the show despite the fact they had been on sale for some weeks and was very disappointed to find they had sold out. She was determined to get into the show even though the manager had explained to her that fire regulations meant that there was a full house, he had already turned away a number of people, and he could not let her in. "Would you come and talk to her?" he asked.

Mediumship requires that I get into a very special 'space' within myself, a very sensitive space, before I begin a show and this requires all my energies and concentration. Before a show I am in no fit space to see anyone so was unable to see the lady. On this occasion the lady's behaviour had clearly upset the hotel staff who in turn had brought their emotions to me. Now I had to ensure these negative feelings did not affect me or they could also affect the show. In my previous work as a bank manager, I had learned how to steel myself to situations I didn't like or that were potentially unpleasant. If I had to tell someone the bank had declined their loan I never enjoyed the experience but I knew it had to be done as part of the job. If the person was upset I could rationalise their reaction and it did not hurt me as I had a defensive shield in place, which protected me. As a medium I must be absolutely open and sensitive – in a space of vulnerability and openness – to make links. If, while I am in such a state someone is angry or hurtful towards me or even if they are going through some emotional situations in their lives, I feel it incredibly deeply – much more deeply than usual, and it can take me a long time to recover. When I return to normal day-to-day functioning, I can deal with aggression and hurtful behaviour as well as most people, but before, during, and immediately after a show I am wide open and completely vulnerable. In this situation I had to contend with the feelings of the lady who wanted to see me, as well as the hotel staff's feelings. I agreed to do a follow-up show at the same hotel within a couple of weeks and the manager thought that that would appease her. Thankfully, it did. It was not a good start to the evening though and I had to work really hard to get myself back into 'show mode'. The old word for medium was 'sensitive' and experiences such as this confirmed why.

In preparation for a show I meditate alone to ensure I am in the right 'space' when the show starts. Meditation helps me to relax my physical body allowing energy to flow freely through me and relax my mind so it is not so busy. In this way I am able to hear the messages between my own thoughts. Meditation also helps me to raise my consciousness and my vibration so that I am closer energetically to the spiritual realms. It is as though their messages are on a different frequency to my own everyday thoughts.

My raw, organic vegan diet is another key factor in getting my vibration closer to the spiritual realms and ensuring that I can attain the right space readily. We are what we eat and if we eat heavy, negatively charged food, that is how we will feel. So I choose to eat vibrant, living food that raises my energy, gives me vitality and stamina and makes my whole body sing. When I look back, I realise that food and nutrition is something I have been interested in for much of my life. As a child my mum would call me her 'little fruit bat' as, left to my own devices, that's exactly what I would eat – fruit and nothing else. The problem was

I didn't leave any for anyone else! As an adult I have tried many different diets along the way; some worked for a time, but I have never felt healthier and more alive than I do when I am eating raw, organic food.

Through meditation and my diet I can maximise my energy levels but I can still only give high-quality mediumship in front of a large group for about two hours at a time. My shows usually start at 7pm and as it gets close to 9:30pm I feel a bit like Cinderella at the ball when the clock strikes midnight. I start to feel my energy level going down and I know I have to bring things to a close or getting the links becomes difficult and the accuracy of the messages is not to my satisfaction It is hard to stop because so many people still want messages and so many in spirit world still wish to communicate, but I have to find a balance.

Just as I need to prepare myself before a show, it is also important for me to close down properly afterwards so that I make the transition to normal functioning. When I first started doing the mediumship shows I found I had awful problems getting to sleep at night – my brain seemed too switched on, too wired, too awake. I have since developed a cleansing and closing down process and sleeplessness has mainly become a thing of the past.

One night I pushed myself too hard seeing a number of people after the show and I drained my reserves just that bit too low. I found myself wide awake in the early hours of the morning, experiencing something similar to a nightmare while still awake. I observed what was happening to me and realised that I was having trouble with someone in 'spirit' who had desperately wanted a message passed on during the show. In the same way that people here wait behind trying to see me after a show, spirit can often do the same.

Spirits often don't mean any harm, they are just really keen to get through to their own loved ones. Initially I found it quite distressing to have spirits try to communicate with me after a show, I mean, what was I supposed to do? How was I supposed to pass on their messages when their loved ones had gone home? It didn't happen too often but often enough to sometimes make me feel as though I had failed in some way. With experience I learnt to ignore these spirits in the knowledge that there are other ways loved ones in spirit can get their messages through if they really want to. When I consciously close myself down it is a bit like closing a door and spirit cannot bother me. The responsibility doesn't always have to rest with me – if I have sincerely done my best at a show I have learned how to let myself off the hook. So it took me by surprise to be having this problem when I had done all my normal closing down rituals. I was confused. Looking back I can only presume that that night I did not have the necessary energy to close myself down properly. The intent to close down had been there but not the energetic strength.

Because I was tired, my own attempts to get the spirit to move on and out of my space were pretty much useless. My energy was lower than the spirit's and because the spirit was emotional he was quite energised and 'winning' the internal battle. How he was feeling was starting to affect me and I was finding it increasingly difficult to separate his feelings from my own. It's a bit like in physical life; if you are really tired and you come into contact with someone who is really angry or frustrated about something you can end up taking on their anger or frustration unconsciously and then later wonder why you are feeling that way. Or if you come across someone who is really down or depressed you too can end up feeling down. Somehow what the other person is vibrating or resonating spills out of their energetic space into yours. In physical life, experience had taught me that another person's emotional state could not affect me as long as I was energised and conscious of what was happening, but that if I was tired or run down I could end up taking on their feelings and emotions. The same principle applies when dealing with the spiritual dimensions.

So in the early hours of the morning, with a persistent spirit playing havoc, I had to ask my partner

Andrew for help. If you don't deal with such situations decisively you run the risk of what most people would describe as a possession – a spirit taking you over. The spirit didn't feel particularly malevolent but I decided not to take any chances. Andrew wasn't too happy about being woken from his sleep but fortunately is very understanding and very knowledgeable about the different dimensions and moving spirits back through to where they need to be. It took about 20 minutes but with Andrew's focus and energy, my energetic space was cleared and the spirit moved on. My head and body felt fully mine again and I was able to get to sleep.

In the morning, which came all too soon, I reflected on what had happened. It had been worth seeing the people after the show but it had clearly taken too much out of me. I made a mental note to limit the number in future. I was glad that I would not have another show for a few nights, as I would need some time to recover. Experiences like this with spirit are not frightening for me because I understand what is happening and I absolutely know that there is nothing to fear in the spiritual dimensions. For someone who doesn't understand what is happening I can see that such experiences could be terrifying and often wonder just how people cope when they start experiencing spirit for the first time. Is that why so many people are diagnosed with mental health problems? Perhaps what we need is more understanding of the spiritual realms, not a fear of them.

As much as I have to get into the right 'space' within myself to do mediumship, I have found that I also need to be in the right 'place'; the actual physical place or venue I'm working in and the equipment I use also needs to be conducive to mediumship. We had a very warm welcome in one particular town with the theatre manager showing us around and taking care of our every need. The theatre was lovely and there was a proper changing room for once – everything seemed to be set up for a good show. I went through my usual preparations getting ready and then meditating. I didn't know I had a problem until I was on stage and trying to pass on the first message. I made a link with someone in spirit world and then found myself losing it again. Something was definitely not right. I checked very quickly if I had a rogue spirit with me – there was no one that I could detect. Perhaps it was just this first link, I reassured myself. The same thing happened with the second link and then third link. I found myself linking with a loved one and then losing the link again. This happened repeatedly. I did not know what was going on. I was a little tired, as we were coming to the end of a long tour but I felt it shouldn't be causing this much difficulty. Andrew came to speak with me in the interval. We had both checked for spirit world interference in our own ways while the first half was underway and we'd both come up blank. It didn't appear to be spirit interference and the audience seemed open and friendly. What was going on? I was getting messages through but they were very hard work.

I went on in the second half still not knowing what the problem was or whether it would persist. Andrew felt it must be that I was just too tired but I knew if I was tired I would have difficulty making the links in the first place. This was different. I could make the links but then I would lose them. It wasn't a lack of concentration, there wasn't anything distracting me and the audience was very attentive. Try as I might I couldn't identify what it was.

When I get a link it is a bit like being pulled towards someone by a magnet; except it is not a magnetic pull, the pull is one of unresolved feelings and love. But as fast as I was pulled to someone and connected with them on this night the connection would fall away and I would lose their loved ones in spirit world. It wasn't a gradual drifting out, it was very sudden – my mediumship was very stop-start. I would get a couple of pieces of information and then lose them and have to reconnect. It was weird. I had never experienced anything like it in nine years of mediumship. I decided to stop trying to analyse and just concentrate on doing the best I could; to be as conscious as I could of what was happening and stay focused on the links. I worked harder than I have ever needed to work, as the links took more energy to make than usual. The people I had passed messages on to were pleased with their messages but I was not. What was I supposed to be learning from this experience? Frustrated does not even begin to describe how I was feeling. I had come so far, practised so much, been open to learn all that the universe had to teach me about spirit communication and here I was feeling like a beginner again, not being able to sustain links.

Two ladies talking to Andrew at the end may have had the answer. They had been amazed that I had done as well as I had as the building was surrounded by heavy-duty wiring for a local radio station. The heavy-duty wires ran all the way around the perimeter of the building and there was a large transmitter for a telephone company on the top of the building. They were impressed that I had managed to work at all with all that electrical interference. Electrical interference had never entered my head – could it affect me? Certainly something had. We couldn't say for sure if that had been the problem with this place but we decided to make sure future venues did not have wires running around them like that just to be on the safe side. Could it be that simple? And if so, why had Spirit not warned me? Why couldn't they have found me a different venue? Even after all my experiences, there are still many questions, and there is still much for me to learn.

One of the worst things for me to deal with during a show is, believe it or not, being in a place that is cold. I didn't realise this until I experienced extreme cold at one show. It was an icy cold day and our show was booked for the evening in the town hall. We called in at lunchtime to see the venue and to ask them to put the heaters on. They did, but with an outside temperature of minus five degrees by the time the show started, it was still freezing. Being backstage was just not an option for me. The backstage walls were brick and there was no insulation or heating. I had to change into my show clothes at the motel and then arrive just before the show was due to start. To do mediumship you have to relax – and relaxing is extremely difficult when you are debilitatingly cold. When the body is cold your muscles tense and your blood vessels constrict to retain body heat. Mind and body are interconnected and if you have ever tried to relax your body while your mind is racing you will know how hard it is to do. With mediumship it is the other way around; a relaxed body helps the mind become clear. If the body is tense the mind is too. I found it hard to make good connections as I just could not relax my body or my mind. At the interval I joined the audience sitting on the small radiators that were working to full capacity but making very little difference to the extreme cold. A local reporter hit the nail on the head when he described the place as 'cold as a morgue'. In the second half of the show I worked wearing my coat, I was warmer and that helped with the quality of the connections but never again. I can only give my best when I am comfortable and warm. I now know to insist on a warm venue!

Experience has taught me that the venue isn't the only physical consideration that has to be taken into account. The nature of the work I do requires very specialised sound equipment. I cannot cope with feedback from microphones in any shape or form as it distracts me and can make me lose a link with a loved one in spirit world. When I am working it is like I am a finely tuned radio receiver receiving information on a particular frequency – while receiving a message I focus on the frequency throughout the message. A feedback whistle, apart from being very painful on the eardrums, takes my attention off the particular frequency I am focusing on and then I have to re-find it. It can be like looking for a needle in a haystack, especially during a show when you have other spirits desperate to get through. The sound quality also has to be good enough for members of the audience who are hard of hearing and not cause feedback from hearing aids, a common problem with some sound systems.

In early shows we had found that we could not rely on the quality of the sound equipment at some places and so had invested in our own. Finding appropriate sound equipment to do all we required was not easy but we eventually found an Italian brand that suited our requirements. It meant that there was extra work for my partner Andrew at each show setting it up, testing it and packing it away but it was better than trying to work with the in-house equipment many of the venues provided, as the quality varied considerably. The Italian purchase proved to be an excellent choice – I could relax knowing that feedback problems from microphones were a thing of the past. All was well until disaster struck.

We had left our precious sound gear in a locked sound room at one venue so we didn't have to pack it up and then bring it back for the second show. When we returned it was not in the room. Our hearts began to race. Perhaps someone had taken it out and put it on stage for us, we thought. But no, there was no equipment on stage and the man in the hall who was helping us set everything up knew nothing about it. The manager of the building was called and other members of staff contacted to make sure the equipment had not just been moved somewhere else by mistake. We tried to stay calm and not panic – the show was due to start in 40 minutes and we had no sound equipment. Phone calls were made and as each person was eliminated we came to the sad realisation that our equipment had been stolen. The police were notified. We were annoyed with ourselves. It was the only time we had ever left our equipment anywhere. We now had just 30 minutes before the start of the show and we could hear the first people starting to arrive in the main hall. The venue was able to lend us their equipment and although it wasn't ideal, it was our only option. Andrew got to work setting things up. I got to work calming myself and letting the situation go. The police arrived at five minutes to seven to take statements. The show started at seven. The timing could not have been worse. All my 'letting go' was in vain – the feelings created in me as a result of the theft were back again, triggered by the police arriving. We did not want to delay the show any longer than was necessary and so we gave the police a brief statement and agreed to go to the police station after the show to finish our statements.

The loss meant we had to then do the show with sound gear that wasn't familiar to us and the microphones had a tendency to make a feedback whistle – the very thing we had eliminated by buying our own equipment. In hindsight, we should have cancelled the show and used the time to sort ourselves out. It had been either cancel or give it your best shot. We chose to give it our best shot. We also chose not to tell the audience what had happened – 'to be professional' – but by the second half I had to explain. The microphones were playing up and I was not in the best place emotionally to make the links. The clairvoyance was easy enough but sustained links with spirit world were few and far between. I like to think that the quality of the show was better than most of the audience would have seen before but part of me also knows that some people only go to see a medium once and I had not been at my best. As a teenager many years ago I had seen a medium at a local hall and had left very dubious about the lady's abilities and feeling conned. I had not gone back and I had not explored the spiritual side of life any further for over 20 years. I know that some people don't come back to see a medium unless they see enough evidence to start them at least asking questions. I had let myself down. I had let spirit world down. Why couldn't I have been more professional and let the stealing of the equipment go? My guides in spirit world were very gentle with me for a few days. I was being taught about how blocks in my emotional energy field can stop a communication with spirit world. I was reminded that I am only human.

Our biggest concern was how we were going to get a replacement sound system for the subsequent shows.

All the shows to follow were in relatively small towns and we didn't consider that they would be big enough to have suitable equipment for hire. What would we do? I could conceivably project my voice, though not perhaps for a full two-hour show. The audience, if they were upset, were sometimes barely audible with microphones let alone without them. Fortunately, the people at the venue agreed to loan us their equipment on a temporary basis. It wasn't ideal, as I had already found, but it was better than nothing. We checked with the two music stores in the town to see if there was anything more suitable and, finding there wasn't, we jumped very quickly at the venue's offer.

The show at the next venue went extraordinarily well despite the fact that I was not the only one 'hearing voices'. Everyone did! Our own system had variable frequencies you could use anywhere. Unfortunately, the system we had borrowed had a fixed frequency, which happened to be the same as the local taxi rank. Nothing was going to stop me concentrating on links, though, and we had an amazing night. There were lots of meaningful messages and lots of laughter, too.

Unfortunately, we never recovered the equipment and had to purchase another set. And yes, much to my embarrassment the police officer did ask me why I couldn't find it myself!

As we have travelled and experienced the day-to-day reality of touring we have found that there are things that can change a potentially suitable place into an unsuitable one. They are wide and varied and difficult to predict or anticipate, as we found in the following experience.

A week or so before the show the theatre manager telephoned me full of apologies. She had only just realised that we would be doing our show on the same night as live boxing was on in the adjacent auditorium. She fully appreciated that the two audiences would be very different. Tickets for our show were going well and it would be difficult to change the date at such short notice. We would just have to work around it. The theatre manager was wonderful and suggested moving us into the main theatre, which was further away from the boxing, at no extra cost. In this way people arriving to see me would not come into contact with the people going to see the boxing and they could have two flows of traffic with two separate entry and exit points. It seemed a good idea. I was not keen on the thought of there being boxing nearby as the energies would be very different to those I used for mediumship and potentially this could cause a problem. There was only one downside to the move: the boxers would need all the changing rooms. I could change in the green room but I would need to use the same corridor as the boxers when I went on stage. I agreed we would still do the show on the planned date but in the main theatre.

As I've explained, I take time to relax, centre myself and meditate before a show and nothing usually distracts me from the task. However, I had never encountered the sound of fists hitting flesh before and its gruesome nature brought me swiftly and abruptly out of my meditative state. The boxing has started, I thought. I knew it would not just be one fight as signs I had seen in the corridor indicated at least 14 different boxers. Cotton wool would have been handy but wasn't something I tended to carry around with me. I could hear every sound and the jeers and cheering of onlookers. It created an 'interesting' energy and I knew I would have to work extra hard with the audience to create the right kind of atmosphere to bring loved ones through. I was bemused that in the same building there would be people looking for peace and people looking for aggression. I looked on the positive side as my Sagittarian optimism often tends to do – it was truly a sign of a free will universe.

I was ready to go. I braced myself. I walked through the corridor the boxers used and onto the stage and thankfully met no one. I explained to the audience that to counter what was going on 'next door' we needed to create a room filled with love and laughter – even more so than usual. I was uplifted by their immediate and overwhelming response. The atmosphere was wonderful and this allowed the messages to come through thick and fast. You had to see the funny and slightly bizarre side of the situation and I joked with the audience that if they did succeed in killing each other next door at least we would be the first to know.

The second half started with question time and there was no shortage of questions after such a successful first half. A young man surprised me by taking the microphone and saying he had come as a reluctant sceptic – his mum had dragged him along. Having experienced the first half he just had to comment on the amount of love he could feel in the room. It was amazing. The audience clapped to show their agreement. As he spoke I saw a young man with him. A good friend who had died quite tragically. I passed on his name. The man in the audience was taken aback and immediately wanted to know how his friend had died.

"Your mum knows," said the spirit nodding at the woman next to him. It had come out of my mouth before I realised what I was saying. Mum nodded.

"You knew and you didn't tell me," he exclaimed to her. It was then that I realised spirit were setting things straight between them and I decided to move quickly on and leave them to it!

The love and support generated by the audience turned this venue with negative energies into a wonderful place and a wonderful show. We should never underestimate the power of people's positive loving thoughts.

I didn't realise when I embarked on my spiritual journey just how much there would be to learn. Every single show I learn something. Sometimes it is about myself, sometimes about mediumship and sometimes about life on the other side. The path isn't easy but I am often overwhelmed by the love and patience that spirit world has for me. Life still has its ups and downs but I know I am supported. I just have to take one step at a time, do my best and leave the rest to them. When something I don't like happens, as happens in life, I am learning not to take it personally. I am learning to look for what it is that I have to learn, even if the lesson is not obviously apparent.

Trusting

Throughout my life as a bank manager, and then more recently as a medium, I have always assessed my own performance. I have been my own worst critic, if you like. In Neuro Linguistic Programming it is called having an internal frame of reference. If we use an internal frame of reference or set of benchmarks for our performance in a particular area it means we decide how well we have done against these. We evaluate our performance. Some of us use an external frame of reference. We assess how well we have done from what others tell us or the reaction we get. Sometimes we may use an internal frame of reference for certain aspects of our lives and an external frame of reference for other aspects.

In terms of my mediumship I have a very strong internal frame of reference; I know how well I have done. I know it because of the strength of energy links: how the hairs stand up on my arms and also through the quality of the information I pass on. I also have an inner voice/guide that tells me how accurate a show or message has been. Even if an audience tells me a show was wonderful, if I do not feel it internally it makes not a jot of difference. The standards I set for myself are very high. In other areas of my life, however, such as choosing something to wear for a special occasion, I may be more inclined to ask a girlfriend or my partner what they think and so use an external frame of reference.

As I've said, at my first large show I was told by my guide that my mediumship was at 75% of my potential. Accuracy of 100% was my goal but it would take a number of significant lessons from spirit world before I made the breakthrough to that level. The first came some months after the first show as I embarked on an extended tour.

For some reason, the adverts for our Wellington shows had not gone into the newspapers in time. When we arrived we found we had sold eight tickets for the first show and just two tickets for the second. I quickly arranged to go on a local radio station to take calls from listeners. On-air mediumship had worked well before, perhaps it would attract a few more people. As we arrived at the hotel that was to be our venue I didn't know to what extent, if any, the radio had helped draw people to the show.

My spirits lifted on entering the hotel venue. It was fabulous. Expansive rooms with luxurious furnishings stretched ahead of us. It would be an ideal setting for the show. The adverts may not have gone in but the venue was perfect. A large spiral staircase led from the ground floor to the first floor where we had hired a large room. Relaxing music from the pianist playing in the bar on the ground floor wafted up the stairs after us creating just the right kind of atmosphere we needed to welcome people to the show. We were similarly impressed by the hotel employees: the staff member appointed to us was excellent and could not do enough for us. We made our usual preparations for the show, enjoying the ambience of the place and at the same time not knowing quite how many people would be there. As I prepared myself in a side room, I decided that no matter how many people turned up it would be my best show ever. I asked internally for help and was shown an image of Sai Baba (the 'avatar' I had visited in India some years previously) walking about. Baba walks very slowly, he almost looks as though he is floating. It felt very unnatural for me to walk as he walked. I had to slow my pace right down. I walked and I walked. In walking so slowly I noticed that my internal state changed, I acquired a 'state of grace'. I could feel the air around me and how I interacted with it really strongly. Andrew came through just before 7pm to see how I was doing and to break the news – there were 16 people in the audience. I presumed that this included the two reporters we had invited to attend. The audience was even smaller than I imagined it would be. I was in safe hands though as I was in a 'state of grace'. I sensed there was going to be a lesson in this for me. I was curious about what it would be.

With an audience of 16 almost everyone is guaranteed a message. There just aren't that many people to choose from. I took person after person up on stage and all the messages were spot on. I didn't think it would be possible for someone to go away from that show without knowing that there was life after death and that I could genuinely communicate with loved ones who had passed over. I mean, it would be hard to have 'plants' in an audience of that size.

I considered that the whole experience of the small audience was to test me to see if I had learned not to judge a situation as good or bad. Could I instead see God/Good in the situation? If I had dwelled on the low attendance, my energy would have spiralled downwards and my mediumship performance would not have been as precise. I had to trust that everything was as it should be for reasons I did not completely understand. It would be six months before I understood why there were so few people there. (Silly me thinking at the time that it was down to the lack of advertising!) What I did not know at that time was that one of the women attending would be significantly placed to help me promote my first book when it was written. Because there were so few people attending, she saw first hand that I was genuine and when the time came she was in the right place at the right time to help my publishers secure a speaking opportunity at the annual booksellers' conference. The booksellers' conference had never had a speaker like me and would perhaps have been hard to persuade without this vote of confidence from within the organisation.

But I hadn't even written my first book at this time – all this was yet to pass. I was just having to trust it was happening for the best.

The show had gone extremely well and I had not let the low attendance get me down. Internally I was satisfied – presumably I had passed the test. I felt confident that we would have a much better audience the following night. After all, I had passed the test as I saw it. Spirit confirmed that I had reached 90% accuracy for the first time. I was so pleased. The size of the audience became unimportant – what mattered was the quality of my mediumship. What would I be like when at 100%? I hardly dared think about it. I had gone from 75% to 90% in a matter of months. Did it mean that 100% would not be that far away?

The next night we went through the usual preparations for the show and I again prepared myself for the show in a side room. Just before 7pm Andrew came through to say we had an audience of just 24 people. Of course, even if last night's audience had gone away raving about the show there were only so many people an audience of 16 people can tell. I returned to my slow walking. Would tonight be as good as the previous one? Was the slow walking the key? Was it this simple? I knew that again I must not let the low attendance get to me and affect my performance.

The show was just as good as the previous night. There were still very few people to choose from so was I being shown that doing smaller shows would improve the quality? Was it smaller shows or slow walking or a combination of both? I didn't know. All I knew was that the two shows in Wellington had been my best shows yet and I was so happy because I felt I had showed beyond doubt to *all* those present that there absolutely was life after death. The feedback from audiences at all of my shows had been very good but I was and still remain my own worst critic. I want to get communication as precise as is humanly possible.

It was at a different venue and city a few months later when I had my first ever complaint about a show. The hotel we were using as a venue rang to let me know they had received a complaint from a lady, whose name was Gloria. Gloria had attended the show the previous evening. She had told the hotel staff that she did not think I was genuine and the hotel staff asked if I would please contact her as they didn't know how to handle her complaint themselves. There had been no other complaints. It took me completely by surprise. No one had ever complained about a show before and what puzzled me was that I considered I had done a good show. I shared the news with Andrew and my friend Lee, who had both been present at the show, and they agreed; it *had* been a good show, not my best but a good show nonetheless. The lady's claims seemed totally unfounded to me. How could she not know I was genuine? I had good links throughout and had given plenty of survival evidence during the show. Again, I knew I had to see the God/good in the situation so I embraced the complaint rather than becoming defensive. If just one person went away feeling I was not genuine or the quality of the mediumship was not high enough, and if Spirit has inspired someone to voice a complaint, perhaps I should listen. I did. I suggested meeting with her at the hotel later in the week, before the next show. Her viewpoint was something I needed to listen to. I was and am totally committed to doing mediumship to the best standard I possibly can.

We met mid-afternoon and got on surprisingly well. So much so that I asked Gloria to come along to my subsequent shows at this venue and let me know what specifically I was doing that was causing the reaction within her that I was not genuine, or not providing good enough proof. I would be doing four shows altogether at the venue so it was an ideal opportunity to get feedback from an independent observer who knew something about spirit communication.

I was unsure what it was I was doing or not doing that had made Gloria feel this way but it certainly got me thinking. The only thing I could think of was that sometimes when making a link with someone and passing on the message you reach a point where the person here can get very emotional. I was tending to back off at that point out of respect for their feelings. I saw their emotion as my cue that they knew absolutely that I had their loved one with me and I didn't need to go further. Perhaps I did need to go further and give even more evidence, not so much for the individual, but from the perspective of the wider audience so that those not receiving messages would know beyond doubt that there was life after death. My audiences were certainly getting bigger. It made sense that if they were all to go away knowing that there was no death my mediumship would need to be stunning.

For the second show I made sure I stayed with each of the connections long enough for there to be absolutely no doubt of who I was talking to in spirit world. A gentleman came through for a lady in the front row – he was speaking a language that I did not understand. From the very beginning of my mediumship, communicating with people of different nationalities has not been a problem as they communicate telepathically – names can be difficult because the sound of them can be unfamiliar to me, but that aside, it is relatively straightforward.

The gentleman was communicating with me to let me know he spoke a different language. I knew it wasn't French, German, Italian, Greek or Spanish, as I could recognise the sounds of all of those. He was from somewhere else. He was standing to the lady's right shoulder indicating to me that he was her father. He seemed quite a formal type of gentleman. The image of him was quite clear to begin with and then he faded away before coming back to the clarity he had begun with. This indicated he had passed away many years ago and that his passing was no longer affecting her as much as it once had. He was very proud of his daughter. I passed on what I was getting to the lady. She was thrilled and explained that her father was Hungarian, which was why I did not recognise the language. Her father talked about his daughter's own abilities and she confirmed she was very spiritually aware herself. Other family members also came through and identified themselves satisfactorily. It gave me confidence knowing that this first message had been to someone well-respected in local spiritual circles and that she had been entirely happy with the content of the message.

Other messages followed including a lady who had taken her own life and a wife who had passed with cancer. Most loved ones in spirit were able to give names and I worked hard to ensure the whole audience had enough proof, not just the recipients of the messages. There were more than the usual tears but it felt that we were with each person as they cried, sharing their experience and their pain, not just observing it. It felt alright to let someone cry. The tears were a release, a healing, and I was reminded of a time when I trained in counselling. One of the first things we were taught was not to hug a person when they cried. The instruction really took me by surprise – it felt natural to me to want to give someone a hug. I remember disagreeing with the trainer who gently explained that the tears are a release and if you hug a person they stop crying and the release stops. "Your 'natural' desire to hug is because you feel discomfort at them crying," she had said. She suggested next time not to give a hug and see what happened. She also took great care to explain that once the release is finished then it is okay to hug. In my counselling work, experience has shown me that this really is the best way but I had just never transferred that knowledge across to my mediumship. I saw for the first time that I had been holding my mediumship back for fear of making people cry – for fear of my own discomfort. I had not been thinking of the recipient of the message or the wider audience at all.

Over the course of this show and the following two shows I worked consciously and conscientiously with my helpers in spirit world. The understanding we developed between us was that the purpose of the shows was to demonstrate to people that there was life after death, that we are eternal. In doing this, those attending would hopefully feel less pain about 'losing' their loved ones and reduce their own fear of dying. The shows would thus reduce pain and fear here. I hoped also that the realisation that there was no death would cause people to start asking themselves questions – and to start pursuing and finding their own truth.

With an average of two hundred people in the audience at each show I could not hope to get a message to everyone. My guides needed to help me find the strongest links, the ones that would be able to give the best survival evidence, so that even if someone didn't get a message they could still leave the show knowing absolutely that there was no death.

I also decided I would be more conscious of everything that I was doing and not doing during the shows and in that state intended to accelerate my learning and my abilities in front of a large audience. I had learned some years ago while on the Neuro Linguistic Programming workshop that maintaining a highly conscious state while I am doing something accelerates my learning – I notice the feedback I'm getting and respond to it moment to moment, second to second, adapting what I am doing accordingly. In this case I would have two kinds of feedback: the internal feeling that made the hairs on my arms go on end and the external feedback of whether the message and details of the loved one in spirit was accepted as correct by the audience member.

The fourth and final show was *stunning*. Every link was clear and precise. Quite early on, the mother of two ladies came through from spirit world. She gave her name and the names of others who were through in spirit with her and details of her passing. One of the daughters on stage with me was wearing Mum's pearls and I found myself pointing at the lady wearing the pearls. Spirit often move my physical body and then I suddenly become aware of what they are doing and realise it is part of the message. "Yes, they are Mum's pearls," the lady confirmed. "Can you look after them better please?" came Mum's light-hearted request. The daughter and her sister laughed. She had nearly lost them earlier that day and that had not been the first time either!

Perhaps the most moving message of the night was for a very young girl whose father came through during a psychometry demonstration where audience members give me pieces of jewellery to hold to assist me in making specific connections with people who have passed over. I found myself looking at my feet and I had a feeling of being pulled down and there was absolutely nothing I could do about it. I felt this in two ways: that I, Jeanette, could do nothing about it and *had* to look down at my feet but also that this gentleman, the father of the young girl, could do nothing about it either. He was being pulled down, but he wasn't panicking. In fact, he was remarkably calm. The young girl confirmed that her father had drowned unexpectedly although he was quite a good swimmer and this had raised questions about his passing. He wanted to put everyone's mind at rest, his daughter's particularly, by clarifying how he had died, and that he had died peacefully.

He also showed me that he was getting through to his daughter in her dreams. She confirmed this. His coming through was not to alarm her but to let her know that he was alright. He was at peace. This message helped her enormously. Dad was worried that she wasn't understanding why he was appearing to her and now she did. Loved ones who have passed over often attempt to come through to us in our dreams. In dream state our brainwaves move into alpha state and on this frequency spirit world are more easily perceived. Sometimes, though, we remember seeing loved ones but not what they said. This was such an occasion.

Over the four shows I had improved my skill level significantly. Internally, I was advised that I was at 90% of my ability at the final show of the four. I considered it was equivalent to my Wellington performances, but the difference was that this had been in front of a larger audience with more spirits to manage. When Gloria came into my dressing room to see me after the show she was amazed at the improvement and she could barely contain herself. "You were on fire, sizzling," and I knew what she meant. I had consciously lifted my own consciousness for the shows and in doing so had raised the quality of spirit communication. We hugged each other. She hadn't known if she would be able to help – but just by making her complaint and being there each night she had inspired me to strive further with spirit communications. What would 100% be like I wondered in my head – I still didn't even know if 100% was achievable.

Personal Growth

When touring I usually do two to three shows each week and so improvements in my skill level are very noticeable when they happen. I didn't know then but it would only be a matter of days after the previous shows before my next breakthrough would come.

My first Invercargill performance had gone very well and I had been happy with the sell-out show. I was hurriedly getting ready for the second show when Andrew came to let me know that it too had sold out. We were both taken aback because both shows had been a last minute addition to our itinerary and had only been advertised the week before. Normally, we advertise a show for three weeks and selling out the first show of 200 people had already exceeded our expectations. Now we had sold out two shows of 200 people without trying. We must be doing something right we felt.

We could only presume that local reaction to the first show was so good that it sold out the second show within hours. I felt truly humble that so many people would want to see me and that Spirit now had the confidence in me to bring so many people and their loved ones in spirit to the shows. I felt overwhelmed and burst into tears. I couldn't seem to stop crying and went on stage with tears rolling down my face and a clutch of tissues in my hand.

The first lady up on stage with me was probably one of the most difficult people I have ever had to deal with during a show. She wasn't giving anything away. The link with her husband and brother in spirit world was strong and I knew it was but she spoke of her brother as though he was still here, which puzzled me initially. I had to decide who to believe – him or her – and I chose him. She had to concede – I was right. The audience loved it. She really pushed me to provide meaningful evidence, although it was all done in a really light-hearted way with lots of humour. I was given proof, after proof, after proof for her. There were many tears of laughter along the way. She was a hard taskmaster but a beautiful soul, and a wise one.

After this first message, all the other links were relatively easy and accurate. I felt my mediumship had moved up to another level. I wasn't given an exact percentage, but I knew it was up from the previous 90%. A new level of confidence accompanied this knowing as well as lots of tears for me and the audience. Increasingly I was recognising that the learning wasn't just about mediumship. In following my chosen path of mediumship I was learning about 'me', becoming more conscious of how I was being and who I was choosing to be. As I became more self aware, I was able to make better choices and that in turn was making me clearer as an instrument for the mediumship.

Andrew and I reflected on what had caused this more recent shift. I had not had time to meditate before the show as I had been swimming with the children. Had the physical exercise helped? It was puzzling. No meditation at all and yet it had been one of my very best shows. Everything was much the same as the previous night, the same venue, a similar audience so why the shift? If anything I would have expected a poorer performance as doing two shows back to back can be tiring, but the opposite had happened.

I replayed the events of the previous evening in my mind and remembered that I had started to cry when I knew so many more people were coming to see me than we had expected. I had felt humbled knowing it was neither me nor the adverts bringing all these people to the shows – it was Spirit. I knew they must put great store in me to do that. I realised I had experienced humility and it had overwhelmed me. I was the messenger but Spirit had to get the people to the shows. I was a small part of a much bigger picture. I was also amazed by the sheer numbers of people needing to know that there is life after death and found myself crying again this time in realisation of the level of pain that people here suffer.

There were a few more weepy days after that as my heart centre opened more than ever before. I was learning to feel ever more deeply how others felt – and it hurt. Did this mean that I would be crying throughout all my future shows? If that was what it took to get the quality up further, I thought, I was game. It would be a small price to pay. Who needs mascara anyway!

With my heart centre more open and my focus fixed on being the best I could be as a medium, my next breakthrough was inevitable. What it would be or when, I did not know but I did know that it would come, it couldn't not. It came, not surprisingly, during the final show of the tour a couple of weeks later.

I had heard nothing but good reports about the hotel venue for the final show of the tour but was still not prepared for what greeted me when I walked into the hotel reception. It was one of the largest hotel reception areas I have ever seen with an impressive sweeping staircase coming down from the first floor and ending with a water feature to the right and a vintage car to the left. The staff were exceptionally helpful and I wished we were staying there ourselves but the hotel had been booked out some time in advance which did not surprise me.

After two days of resting and enjoying the sun before show night my energies were back up to where they needed to be. I wanted the last show of the tour to be a superb one but I knew it wasn't only down to me. When I heal, my desire to help someone get well makes not a jot of difference. In some ways it can actually get in the way. If I am desperate for someone to be healed, say a child, I feel my desire inside like a twisting energy and it conflicts with and can stop the healing energies that are very open and flowing. In much the same way my desire to put on a good show with top quality evidence makes not a jot of difference.

Experience has taught me that expectations can limit our experiences here. I have a part to play to make sure I am healthy, happy, relaxed and open but I leave the rest to unfold – I leave the rest to Spirit/Life, if you like.

What happened at the show was totally unexpected. I reached 100% of my ability. Why this show specifically? I do not know. It was partly down to me – I was in the right space with no expectations. Partly the success of the show was down to the audience as they were open and friendly and receptive to what I had to say and partly it was down to Spirit. There were a number of loved ones in spirit world who had passed 'before their time' and the uniqueness of their passings coupled with their sheer will-power to get through to their loved ones was a powerful combination. The diversity of messages was incredible.

I smiled at a lady in the audience to make eye contact. I could see that she was eager for a message.

"I have your mum with me," I said.

The lady in the audience confirmed, "Yes, my mum has passed over."

Two large male figures came close in on either side of her mother in spirit. "She has your two sons with her," I carried on. The look of relief on the lady's face was visible for all to see. The 'boys' towered above me and their nana. I described what I was seeing. "I can see your mum and your grown sons are towering above her – one of them is ruffling Nana's hair."

"They were both big," the lady explained, "and they used to do just that to my mum." It was wonderful proof but they hadn't finished. I was shown that the sons had both died in road accidents. I passed this on. "Yes, that's right, they did," came the response.

"Two separate accidents, and neither was their own fault," came out of my mouth.

"You are exactly right!" Mum exclaimed. She was clearly thrilled that her loved ones had come through and also that they had been able to give such significant evidence. All three were doing well on the spiritual side of life.

I barely had a chance to recover from that message before Spirit came in and all but took me over as I was walking down the aisle. It was as though my feet were being lifted off the floor. My attention was pulled to the gentleman on my immediate left. He didn't look at me initially but I just had to look at him. This message was for him and it was definitely coming through. I quickly realised that I had his son in spirit world with me. He confirmed yes, he had lost his son and said no more. He looked back in front of him and didn't make eye contact with me. I could see he needed his proof and was choosing not to give anything away. I could feel my feet lifting off the floor again. I knew the deceased son was giving me this feeling to let me know how he had died.

"Did your son's feet lift off the floor as he died?" I asked.

Retrospectively, it sounds a silly question and reading this you can probably guess how he died – but when I am totally connected with Spirit I am not using my logical brain, I am just passing on what I see, sense or experience. With hindsight I feel quite embarrassed about asking such a question.

"Yes, my son's feet would have come off the ground when he died," came the measured response. The man paused before continuing, swallowing emotion, "My son took his own life by hanging himself."

147

How did I not see that one coming? The son was really very sorry for what he had done but he hadn't seen another way forward. He knew his death, particularly the way that he passed, had caused much pain and he was sorry. He also wanted his dad to know he was alright and not as troubled as he had been when he was here.

Precise message after precise message came through. The audience was spellbound and so was I. A workmate who had died quite suddenly popped in to let his colleague know he was safely on the other side now. A lady's husband came through to talk about his funeral. "They were going the wrong way," he said, shaking his head and laughing. His wife confirmed that her husband's body had mistakenly been taken to the wrong cemetery. She was pleased to hear that her husband had seen the funny side.

Every message was accepted in its entirety and for me it was magical to observe just how well mediumship can be done when everything comes together. It opened my eyes to what was possible. I had never seen mediumship like this before; not even on television.

Perhaps the sweetest message was for a gentleman whose much-loved wife had passed with cancer. He had helped look after her when she was sick and neither of them were very old. Throughout the message the deceased wife repeatedly took over my right arm and pointed at her husband's chest. I asked the gentleman if there was anything wrong with his chest and he said no. Still the pointing went on but it was getting ever more insistent. I tried to finish the message and move on, but no, she insisted that I ask him *why* she was pointing to his chest. I wanted my arm back and so I did as she asked.

"Okay, I give up," I finally said. "Can you understand why your wife keeps pointing at your chest?"

"Yes, I think I can" he admitted.

"Please tell me what it means," I said handing him a microphone. The audience waited with anticipation.

He took a deep breath and for a split second it looked as though he was going to say 'no' but he didn't, he put his embarrassment to one side and bravely shared with us all what he thought it meant.

"Before coming to the show tonight I dabbed a little of my late wife's perfume on my chest," he said with some embarrassment, "...and no one else knows I did that."

"No one apart from me," said his late wife, with a smile, in my head. It was lovely proof, proof he could not deny. It was what he had needed. His late wife had been with him when he thought of her as he put the perfume on and would always be with him whenever he thought of her. The gentleman's wife in spirit was satisfied that she had made her point and peacefully pulled back from me. The mystery had been solved and my right arm was mine once more.

I often wonder how I would feel receiving a message like that. Something that only I knew about. It struck me it was the very best kind of evidence. It was the kind of proof I would want if I was on the receiving end of a message. I asked spirit world for more like that. After all if we don't ask we don't receive!

As always at the end of the show there were people to see but this time Spirit had guided me to see a particular lady. During the second half of the show I had started to link with her and was then told very clearly to see her, her husband and daughter at the end and in private.

At first I didn't understand why but as soon as we went into the private room and a young man hopped into my body, I did. He gave me his name and I passed it on. He was their son and brother respectively. I looked down at my physical body and for the first time realised that my legs were astride and I was holding onto something with each hand. It is funny how spirit world can do that to me – I notice after the event that I am standing or sitting differently. Mum confirmed that their son had died on a motorbike. Of course, now that she said it I could see my hands were in a position consistent with holding handlebars, and my legs were astride in the same way that they would be if I was on a motorbike. As with the case of the young man earlier in the evening, I felt awfully silly not realising something so obvious at once but as I said before I am so focused on being open that my logical brain isn't working.

In this case their son and brother was able to give his family the much needed evidence that he was safe and well in spirit world and the names of relatives they knew, who were looking after him. The son had wanted to get through but hadn't wanted me to pass the message on during the show as he was worried about how his dad would respond to a message. He didn't want to make his dad cry in public. In private they could all shed their tears freely, and hug him through my physical body, once more. I cannot explain how I feel at times such as this. I feel truly blessed to be part of such very special moments. My life is truly worthwhile. *Exquisite* is the best word I can find to describe how I feel – I can't imagine anything beyond this.

I was thrilled by the quality of mediumship I observed myself doing at this show. I reaffirmed to myself and my guides that this was the level I want to work at consistently from now on. A level where there is no room for doubt. The best news was that my guides confirmed that for the first time I was at 100% of my ability.

Spirit world was supporting me to the highest possible level. I couldn't help wondering, 'Would I now stay at this level or would there be other lessons for me to learn?'

Proof

Unless of course they are journalists, sceptics do not usually come for a private consultation. And journalists think we don't know this! However, at the shows you do occasionally find the odd sceptic in a large audience. Usually, they have come to support a family member or friend who desperately wants to believe in an afterlife. I regard them as having good intentions – making sure that their loved ones are not being misled or conned. I say this from the position of being the biggest sceptic I knew for the first 31 years of my life. I know how sceptics think and that has served me well in approaching the whole concept of proof.

You would think spirit world would keep me away from the sceptics but quite the opposite. If sceptics have come to a show, spirit world endeavours to give them a message and to at least challenge their beliefs. One such gentleman came to one of my early shows. Earlier in the evening, I had taken his wife on stage and passed on messages from both her mother and her father, which she had been very happy with. Later when I tried to pass by where they were sitting in the audience, I was strongly drawn to the lady's husband. I didn't know just how sceptical he was until I was well into the message.

As I linked with him I was able to tell him that I had his mother in spirit with me.

"That's right, but then at my age (mid-50s) you might expect that," he confirmed jokingly.

His mother told me that her name was Mary.

"Yes," he conceded. "But Mary is a common name," he added sceptically. "We cremated her a couple of years ago," he continued.

"No, he didn't!" came Mary's indignant response. "I was buried." Mary was strongly disagreeing with her son in my head.

How would I tackle this? "Are you sure you cremated her?" I enquired gently. "You didn't *bury* her? Because she seems to be telling me you did."

There was an awkward silence. "Oh my goodness! You are right. I had forgotten; we *did* bury her," the man admitted, somewhat red-faced. The audience collapsed into fits of laughter. Mary had helped me to lighten a tense moment. This information was wonderful proof for the sceptical son that Mary, his mother, was alive and well in the spiritual side of life and that maybe there was something more to this than he had first thought.

It is 10 years now since I first awoke spiritually in the UK and went from being a sceptical bank manager to being able to experience spirit world first hand. My experiences changed my life and my outlook on life, or rather my outlook on life became more open and that in turn allowed me to have the experiences I have had. I was told very strongly right at the beginning of my awakening that I was here to 'give people proof'. I still smile to myself and cringe a little when I think back to an experience very early on where I stood by the lake in Regents Park thinking that walking on water was what I had to do to give proof. I had told the trainer of the Neuro Linguistic Programming workshop I was attending that I was here to 'give people proof' and he had challenged me to prove it. The proof he had wanted to see was me walking on water. So there I was, standing by the lake, wanting to give the trainer his proof but not daring to step out onto the water. As this story illustrates, I did not understand how I would be giving proof or what I would be giving people proof of to begin with. No wonder spirit world didn't let me out on an unsuspecting public for several years. I had much to learn before I could be entrusted with that role. Even now, I know that my role here is still unfolding, there is still much I have yet to discover about myself and about 'life'. Over the years I have come to the conclusion that the proof I am here to give is partly proof that we do not die; that there is an afterlife. More significant than this, however, is a larger proof that we are much more than we yet consider ourselves to be.

What constitutes real proof in terms of showing that a person did not die and that there is an afterlife? To me it is a combination of information. The sceptic in the earlier story was quite right, giving the name Mary in itself means very little. In an audience of 200 a great number of people will be able to accept the name Mary in spirit world. Sceptics are right when they say that mediums who throw common names to a large audience may not be proving mediumship as much as they are proving the law of probability. So what level of information takes it beyond the law of probability to absolute proof?

For a start, I always go to the individual, not an area of the audience. I hold the view that if the message is for you, surely your loved ones in spirit world can at least point you out to the medium. If they can't, I personally would question the message. Giving the name or names of spirits is vital but these are only significant if they are given to the individual and not to a group of people. I also give the relationship of the spirit to the living person. This is especially important if it is a common name but it is something I do as a matter of course. This greatly decreases the odds that I have selected it by chance. In the sceptic story I was able to tell the gentleman his mother had passed and that her name was Mary – a good start but for me that was still not good enough. Putting my sceptical hat on – I could take the view that somehow that information could have been researched before the show without the gentleman's knowledge. (You see I can be a very good sceptic when I want to be.) I don't ever research audiences nor do I have someone do that for me. I don't need to. Spirit world give me all the information I need and the mediumship is best when I know absolutely nothing about the person I go to in the audience. So although I had his mother's name I needed something else, something definitive. Something that I could not reasonably know. Mum arguing with her son when he said she was cremated did it. The information was specific and was not something *I could have known*. The way it blurted out of me was also very real. She was, through me, arguing back and I suspected she had not been one to mince her words when she was here.

For real proof then, I want their name, their relationship to the living person, how they passed, when they passed and significant information about them that I could not possibly know – the quirkier the better. Information that is not even known to other family members is the icing on the cake though sometimes, because of the sensitivity of the information, this has to be passed on privately. I try not to be too prescriptive about the proof and be open to whatever combination of proof comes. Sometimes, for example, spirits are just unable to give me their name and if I kept holding out for it there would be a long silence and my holding out for a name would temporarily block all the other information that was coming through that might be suitable 'proof'.

Here are a couple of examples of messages with good proof from the many I could share.

A Dutch gentleman came through at one show to talk to his two daughters who were in the audience. I invited them up on stage with me. For some reason, as I was talking with him and passing on his message, he wanted to keep giving them tomatoes. Tomatoes seemed a strange thing but I know now that even the strangest message has a meaning for those receiving it. Finally I decided to ask why he would be wanting to give them tomatoes. Both daughters agreed that if he was still here he would be doing exactly that. He was a keen gardener, he had never given them flowers in their lives but he was always giving them tomatoes that he had grown in his garden. Simple proof yet effective and it was unlikely to fit anyone else in the audience, especially when it was given with the combination of other information that had preceded it.

Close to the end of another show I was drawn to a lady and her daughter sitting towards the back of the room. The lady offered me a beautiful pendant on a chain to hold, to assist me in making a connection with her loved one. Immediately I felt two spirit beings with me – the lady's mother and father. I communicated this and the lady confirmed that yes, both her parents had passed away. She wasn't that old and the physical me was surprised that she had lost both her parents. Her father then went to stand behind his granddaughter. He told me very proudly that she had been named after him. I noticed he had an unusual accent, one I didn't recognise. How could his granddaughter be named after him? It didn't seem to make sense to me. However, I knew that despite this it was probably right. Spirit don't usually get it wrong, as in the last example.

I said, "Your father tells me that your daughter, his granddaughter, is named after him. Is that right?"

The lady beamed. I passed her the microphone so that she could explain to the rest of the audience. The lady explained that her parents were Latvian. (No wonder I didn't recognise the accent!) Her daughter was named after both her mother and her father. The lady had taken letters from each of their names to make up a unique and very special name for her daughter. It was a piece of information that I could not possibly have known and confirmed for her that I was in fact communicating with her deceased parents. It was a lovely ending to the show and reminded me how ingenious spirit world can be when giving survival evidence.

Some sceptics say that mediums read body language. You bet I do! I was trained in it while working for the bank. I use body language to gauge a person's receptivity and sensitivity to a message but I don't use it to *get* a message. If you watch my body language when I am connecting with Spirit and receiving a message you will see that I am somewhere else – my consciousness is in the spiritual dimensions, my eyes almost glaze over and it is clear that I am often not even looking at the person. I would love to hear how I could use the observation of body language to get Dad's name or how Mum died.

The argument that mediums read body language is also well and truly negated, in my case at least, because I can give accurate messages to people when I take live calls on radio or television.

My first experience of live mediumship on radio was in the UK. I wondered if it would be just the same in New Zealand and was a little apprehensive as I made my way into a New Zealand radio station for the first time. The radio station was situated upstairs above another shop and I was pleased to find that the station looked very much like a UK station, albeit smaller. The working practices also seemed similar, except there were fewer adverts and more technology, which surprised me.

But then it had been a good five years since my radio work in the UK. The lady announcer was very friendly and informal and she seemed genuinely interested in what I did. She helped me to relax straight away and we chatted on air about how I came to be working as a medium. In no time at all I was ready to take calls.

I love doing radio shows for a number of reasons. Firstly, they enable me to reach a wider audience than I would ordinarily get access to. People who may not come to see me at a show may hear me on radio. Secondly, they enable me to show that I can in fact talk to the dead. A sceptic may say that I have plants in a live audience or that I am reading a person's body language but on radio both arguments are not valid. The radio station selects which calls are put through to me – I have no input into the selection of callers so there are clearly no plants and I am not able to see the callers so reading body language is out of the question. So how then do I do it? How can I give telephone callers names of loved ones and unique details about them? It amazes and impresses most people and even other psychics have expressed their complete amazement to me that I even attempt to go on radio and talk to spirit world. It never entered my head that I wouldn't be able to do mediumship on radio. There is no secret to doing it on radio. I do it in the same way I do it at the shows or in private consultations with someone.

Our loved ones in spirit world no longer have physical bodies and so they are no longer limited in time and space as we are. They can be with a caller on the other end of a phone and then link with me when I accept the call and start paying attention to the caller's voice. It is not difficult, but it does take a lot of energy and I have to focus intently.

Even on radio our loved ones in spirit are keen to give us the proof we need that they are still with us as the messages they give me to pass on to the callers demonstrate. On one particular station I remember taking a series of calls in quick succession. It is very tiring to work in this way and so I usually limit the time I spend in radio stations to an hour at most. A record played between messages to let me clear each group of spirits before the next ones come in. I had taken several calls and had been able to tell the callers details about their loved ones who had passed over. For one lady, I was shown by her grandmother that she had had recent trouble with a car door. She laughed when I told her this. "I sure have. I fell out of a car when the door didn't lock properly. I have just returned from two weeks in hospital." Grandma in spirit had found just the right thing to say to let her granddaughter know that she really was still around.

My freakiest experience on radio began with me talking on air with the two radio announcers about my change of life from bank manager to medium and then moved on to taking calls from listeners. As soon as I started I got the same reaction from the announcers that I have had from many around the country 'how do you do that?'. You could almost see their minds ticking, trying to work it all out. Logic couldn't explain to them how I was able to tell people information about themselves and their loved ones just from the sound of their voice on the telephone. They were choosing who I spoke to and often amongst the callers would be one of their regular callers or someone they knew, so they knew that it wasn't being set up. I smiled to myself. It would be interesting to see how they felt at the end of the show.

The next call I received was from a young lady and the quality of the sound suggested she was calling from a car phone. Immediately I felt her grandfather with me.

"I have your grandfather with me. He says he has not been passed over very long, just a few days."

"You are so right," came the young lady's voice. "We are just on the way to the funeral!"

The radio announcers were white and I think I was too. Nobody spoke and you could have heard a pin drop in the studio. I suddenly realised I had forgotten to ask for Grandfather's name! But it didn't matter, sufficient proof had already been given. The announcers played a couple of records back to back and once we had all recovered from the shock I was ready to take a couple more calls. That one had made the hairs on the back of our necks stand on end. I love going on radio. It really does make people think; especially those who would not normally come to one of my shows, and especially the radio announcers who know first hand that it is for real and invariably want me back.

Radio is not the only medium that spirit world has drawn me to. As part of the promotion for my first book *Medium Rare*, I was invited to appear on nationwide morning television. My life story, detailed in the book, is intriguing but the idea of live mediumship on television captured their imagination and they arranged for me to take phone calls live on air from callers I had not met before. They didn't let me know in advance that this was what they would be doing. As far as I knew officially, I was just going in to talk about my book but thankfully spirit world did let me know what would be happening. Spirit world said that the TV station would 'surprise' me when I arrived by asking me to take live calls. I was not to be concerned, however, because it wasn't television's idea, it was spirit world's – they had dropped the idea into somebody's head at the station. It would be alright – everything would be taken care of for me. I was glad they were so sure – I wasn't.

It was my first live TV appearance so it was all pretty nerve-wracking for me – would it work like it did on radio? Or would I need to do something differently? As I've already indicated in previous chapters, I have to be relaxed to get the messages through clearly. Would the nerves affect me? They were my biggest worries. I realised I would only get one shot at it and it could make or break my career.

You can imagine my absolute relief when I connected strongly with the deceased father of the very first caller. Yes, it did work the same as radio and live performances and once I was underway any nervousness I was feeling disappeared. I couldn't get the name of the caller's father because he was Maori and I couldn't recognise the name but I was shown that he died very suddenly. A lot of men do, a sceptic would say, and they would be right. Next I was shown that he died *on* a plane. I wasn't shown a plane crash just that he died *on* a plane. Even a sceptic would have to admit that dying on a plane was a much less likely way of passing. Dying on a plane that didn't crash was even more unusual.

I was shown that there were lots of people worrying about him or initially not knowing whether it was him who had died and then they were worrying about where his body was. I relayed these feelings to the caller and as much information as I could make sense of as it came to me. She just listened as I shared. When I finished she clarified for me and all those watching what had happened. It turned out that her father was on a plane and had had a heart attack. A large gathering of people was waiting for him to arrive for a meeting on a marae. When he did not arrive they sought information from the airline. There had been a long period where they didn't know what had actually happened, if it was him that had died or another passenger and then when they found out it was him they couldn't track down his body. It had been taken somewhere and no one they spoke to knew where. This caused a lot of distress to his wife and the rest of the family.

The atmosphere in the studio was electric as I suspect it was in many living rooms across the country. I know there were a number of sceptics amongst the TV crew and the viewers who had their beliefs shaken that morning. All my information had been correct. What are the odds of guessing all that? I only had the caller's voice on the end of the phone to listen to and the TV company determined who they put through to me. I was on the show for an hour and 45 minutes and the station received over 52,000 calls from people wanting to speak to me. So the odds of me taking that particular call were over one in 52,000. The odds of me getting all the information I did correct – incalculable. Spirit world clearly intended for me to be successful that day despite my nervousness. Somehow they got that particular call put through to me first, so that I would then be able to relax. I was reminded that I am very much their instrument. All I need do is be calm, open and relaxed. They will do the rest and it will be better than I could ever imagine. Just like life really!

Even the most sceptical of reporters sometimes gets affected when spirit world is keen to give someone proof. One reporter I came across at a show was keen to have his own proof. When someone is strongly sceptical their energy field is often closed, making it hard to connect with their loved ones. Fortunately in this instance, he had his sister with him at the show and I was able to pass a message to her instead. Afterwards he said he didn't know how I did what I did, but he was impressed. In a subsequent article he said he thought I might be mind-reading. However, he also conceded that the ability to mind-read would probably be even more remarkable than mediumship.

Could it be that I am mind-reading? I did consider this in the early days. Could I just be picking up old memories? But the spirits I see are very 'real' and I *know* it's not mind-reading because there have been many times where I have passed on information and the person has had to go away to check it out. A recent example was when a lady brought along a watch on behalf of her brother-in-law. As I held the watch, her own father came in first – he was blowed if the brother-in-law's father was going to get in first! His daughter was the one who had paid for the ticket and so Dad was coming in first. "Brother-in-law should have come along himself if he wanted a message," blustered Dad. Dad passed on his message to his daughter and then I quickly passed on information for the absent brother-in-law from his father in spirit. The lady came along again to a subsequent show and she publicly relayed what had happened previously and confirmed that all the information I had given to her for her brother-in-law had proved to be correct. In this case the lady did not know whether the information was correct until she checked with her brother-in-law, so I couldn't be reading her mind.

A big turning point for me in terms of giving people proof came in 2004 when I was interviewed by a widely respected, investigative journalism television programme. Part of the show was about me, my family and my life story. As the filming went on, they asked me if I would be prepared to be 'put to the test' and we talked about what a fair test would look like. To me it made no sense to pass on messages to the interviewer or their crew as a sceptical person could say that I had investigated them before they arrived. I suggested that they find me a selection of people, that they had chosen, who had lost loved ones and see what I was able to ' each of them. They jumped at the chance and within the week took me to a secret location to meet three people I had never met before. This guaranteed that there were no plants or setups – I was on my own. My only concerns were that I had no control over how open the people they selected were nor how strong their connections to their loved ones in spirit world would be.

I was very nervous when the day came. I was introduced to the three people together and told their first names. The cameras were rolling. I couldn't do all three at once, I quickly explained. The spirits would get jumbled. I would need to see them one at a time. The cameras were turned off, the seating rearranged and the first lady brought in. They filmed me as I connected with each person in turn. I will start with the gentleman I saw second and you will see why shortly.

The second subject was a gentleman who by his own admission was quite sceptical and was very difficult to connect with. Even so I could see that he had his grandfather on his dad's side with him. His grandfather gave me the name William and yes, he confirmed that was his name. It is possible I just got lucky but unlikely. Grandfather was showing me sticks.

"No," said the gentleman "that didn't mean anything." A few moments silence and then grandmother was there too – they were her sticks. "Yes," he conceded, "that made sense." There were a couple of pieces of information that weren't understood by him and then I was shown keys – car keys. I asked him if he had just purchased a new car. This rocked him a bit because sure enough he had. He just couldn't explain how I knew that. It surprised me that it was this final piece of information that made him think there may be something more to this than he had thought. The chance of someone having bought a new car are surely more likely than the chance of someone being able to name your paternal grandfather, but I guess what is proof to one person is less significant to another.

The third subject, a lady, had her father with her. He gave me the name Edward.

"Close," she conceded, "my dad's name was Edwin."

I was shown that:

Dad died suddenly – he did.

That he collapsed – he did.

That Mum found him – she did.

That when she found him Mum flapped around not knowing what to do – she did exactly that.

That she then worried that she hadn't done the right thing – exactly right.

After that a small dog scratching at the door and trying to get in to the room distracted me and I lost the clarity of the link.

These examples showed the viewing public that the odds that I 'know' these things by chance or through mind-reading or body-language are pretty slim. But just to be absolutely sure, Spirit arranged for me to receive the story I will share with you now. It was actually the first of the three readings I did but when you read it you will understand why I have left this one until the last, and why the television company played it last in their programme and aired it in its entirety – completely unedited. They wanted the viewers to see the complete clip and they left it to the viewers to make their own judgements.

The subject was a lady of roughly the same age as myself. She had her mother in spirit world with her very strongly and when I held Mum's ring the connection intensified. I couldn't get a name. Instead emotion came flooding through. The connection was clear, almost too clear, and what I saw next was both graphic and disturbing. First, I saw an open palm covered in blood, and felt eyes looking at the palm. The internal thoughts and feelings were very distressed – 'there's blood on my hands'. Then I could see lots of blood everywhere, just lots and lots of blood all over. I felt the awful feelings her mother felt as she died – both the physical and emotional feelings. It was as if it was me – I was overwhelmed with emotion at what I was seeing and the feelings I was experiencing. I wasn't shown a murder and I wasn't shown a suicide. In my head I couldn't work it out – there was so much blood it looked like a murder scene but I had not been shown a murder or a murderer. I was so emotional, the crew stopped filming for a while and Andrew came over to take the ring out of my hand. I just wanted to hug the daughter. I knew she had found the body and that she had kept much of it all to herself. She had been so brave.

We were taken into an adjoining room while the daughter was interviewed for her reaction to what had happened. When the TV crew returned they were white but they didn't let on how accurate or not my message had been. My head and heart were still racing – I still didn't fully understand what I had seen. It had been gruesome. Should I have continued? Was it a murder? Did they need to find the murderer?

I needed about an hour to sort myself out before I could continue with the other subjects. Andrew and I went outside for a walk. "What was it you saw?" he asked.

"I don't know," I said, frustrated that I didn't know how her mum had died. I just knew that there had been lots and lots of blood and that the daughter had had to deal with it all.

"But do you think it was a murder?" Andrew gently pushed.

"I don't know. I didn't see a murder taking place or a murderer, or a weapon," I said. "Could it have been a suicide?" Again, I didn't know. I didn't see slashed wrists. She was remorseful but not suicidal as far as I could tell.

We walked and talked and gradually I was able to clear all the residual thoughts and feelings from my space. I knew I had to go on with the remaining two subjects to complete the test. I got myself into the best mental space I could and went through with them. Although the evidence was not as good as I would have liked, as you have already read, there was still significant information that could not have been obtained by chance.

I didn't find out the full details of what had happened to the first subject's mum until much later. This was the daughter's explanation of what happened: It had been her birthday and her mum hadn't called her as she usually did and so she went round to see her. As she opened the door there was blood up the hallway and on the walls. There was blood everywhere in the room and her mother's dead body. She picked up the phone to call for help and she got blood on her hand – it had really shaken her when she realised she had her mum's blood on her hand – and that was what I started to see psychically when I first took the ring. The emotions and the anguish I felt were Mum's feelings as she lay there dying and reflecting on her life. It had all been too much for me – too much to bear and I think it had been too much for Mum. It looked 'like a murder scene' and at first that is exactly what the police thought too but it transpired that it wasn't. The poor woman's death was slow and painful – she had a very rare medical condition that caused her to bleed from every orifice. The chances of dying in this way are literally millions to one – so how could I pick up on it like I did? And what are the odds of me guessing that when I have never met the lady before in my life? The daughter knew beyond doubt that I had connected with her mother but it was a traumatic ordeal for all of us, the film crew included. It was, however, awesome proof.

With every show and every message I am constantly refining what I do. I take the responsibility of what I do very seriously. There are not that many people here on the earth (just yet) able to prove the existence of an afterlife as well as I do and so every communication is important and is an opportunity for me to learn and improve.

I believe it is in the interests of all concerned to keep raising the standard of proof for mediumship. If we ask consistently for proof, spirit world and/or the universe will give it in the best way they can. Sceptics serve the psychic community well by challenging us to do better and be more precise with the information we are bringing through and I see that as very positive. They inspire me to do the best I can on a consistent basis and I have much to be grateful to them for. I have to say though, there are significantly fewer sceptics crossing my path these days and a number of ex-sceptics have become very good friends.

Three Generations Try to Help

For every person in the audience, there are usually five or six loved ones wanting to come through. One of my key jobs is to identify which are the strongest links to communicate with and which are the most important links that need to be made. The two are not necessarily the same, as this story indicates.

George, quite a strong character in spirit world, pulled me over to a lady sitting a few rows back in the audience. As I walked over to her I asked if she understood who George was. He looked like a father figure to me judging by his age. The link was strong and so I was quite taken by surprise when she said, "No, the name George doesn't mean anything to me." George was persistent and all pervading. He held my attention tightly with her and I found myself getting closer and closer to her until I was closely examining the golden chain around her neck.

"That chain you are wearing was his!" I exclaimed, matter-of-factly jabbing my finger at it so forcefully

I was in danger of touching it and her. George was clearly in charge of what was happening. A part of me watched in wonderment at the scene unfolding before me.

A sudden flash of realisation swept across the lady's face, "Oh yes, it *was* George's chain." An expression on the lady's face of 'how could she know that?' was quickly followed by 'how could I *not* remember George?'. The well-dressed lady explained that George had in fact been her father-in-law. "I was only thinking of my immediate family," she explained, clearly flustered at not recognising the name earlier.

In-laws can and do come through on a regular basis. Usually they come through when there is either unfinished business, something is left unsaid, or to bring through their child; the partner of the person who has passed. I suspected I was dealing with the latter but hadn't yet got a strong enough link with her partner to be sure. "Would you like to join me on stage?" I asked hopefully. Moving away from the rest of the audience and their loved ones in spirit, to the stage, would make the rest of the communication easier, and this would be important especially if it turned out to be her husband and/or an emotional link. The lady nodded agreement, the audience applauded and in no time at all we were settling ourselves into the chairs on stage. I poured us both a glass of water and the audience became silent, patiently waiting for the rest of the message.

It is quite common for an older spirit to come through first when I make a connection. It may be that they are particularly strong-willed and can use this to help maintain a link. Or it may be that they have been in spirit world longer and so have a better understanding of how things work from that side. As I had suspected, George was not the main link, even though he was a strong one. There were at least one and possibly two other males in view, both younger than George, but standing back from the proceedings. My instincts told me that they really wanted to come through but they were just biding their time; everything in due course. The strength of this first gentleman's spirit was what had caught my attention amongst all the other spirits vying for attention. George was simply playing his part and getting me to link with this particular lady. He would likely now help bring through the others.

As soon as we had both settled and relaxed, George confirmed my feelings by bringing through Colin. Colin was his son and the lady's husband. "George is bringing through a man called Colin." I barely had time to finish what I was saying when she confirmed, "Yes, Colin was my husband." She was clearly taken aback at the quick change from George to Colin. I explained to the audience that George had been in spirit world longer than her husband and that this was why he had come through first. "George was also particularly strong-willed and confident," I said. "You can say that again," she said laughing.

Colin immediately told me he had a problem with liquid – he burped an alcoholic burp and I carefully chose to convey the specific words he had used. I knew there was a good reason for this. "Can you understand Colin telling me that he had a problem with liquid?"

"Absolutely! He was an alcoholic," came the frank and honest response. That was the impression he had clearly given me but it hadn't been my place to bring it out into the open. I was glad of the lady's candour as it would make relaying the rest of the message that much easier. Colin hadn't wanted to let everyone in the audience know that he had been an alcoholic but it was alright if she told them. It was then her choice.

Colin shrank in size in my internal vision. He bowed down his head and wrung his hands in remorse and regret. The word 'mortified' popped into my head, he nodded and internally I was shown his funeral. Piecing it together I realised that he was telling me that he was mortified about what happened at his funeral. When I relayed this I could see from the lady's fervent nodding that I had really touched a nerve; the audience was hanging on every word. Colin wasn't wasting any time. He had gone straight to a big issue that needed to be healed. "He is so sorry about what happened at his funeral. He is bowing his head in shame and guilt and remorse."

Colin was pushing me to convey how dreadful he felt about the whole situation – his alcoholism and whatever it was that had happened at his funeral. The lady lost no time in explaining. At the funeral her husband's friends, who also had alcoholic tendencies, had blamed her for her husband's death and it simply wasn't true. A horrible accusation to cope with at any time let alone at the funeral when there is so much to deal with. Now we could all understand why he was so shame-faced about the situation. Colin just wanted her to know that he was sorry for his 'friends' behaviour, their cruel words and that their view was not his view.

I had barely finished relaying Colin's feelings when everything shifted within me, the remorse and anguish disappeared and in its place was love. At first I thought that the communication had healed something between them and I was seeing a shift within Colin, but no, Colin had disappeared. He and the remorse and anguish had gone and had been replaced with a much younger man and love.

I knew the whole mood of the message had shifted and I think the audience sensed it to. "I have a younger man with me now," I explained. The whole mood and pace of the communication had become more sensitive. "He tells me his name is Glenn." Then 'accident' came into my head, loud and clear. "It seems he died in an accident," I interpreted. There were immediate tears from the lady on stage with me and I took a moment just to give her some time. This was the loved one she wanted to hear from more than anyone else. George had been strong and forceful and determined to get through but he wasn't the one she really wanted to hear from. Her husband had been a good link too but this third link was special and very loving. The hairs on my arm were on end. This was the *important* link. It brought tears to my eyes and I could tell that even though I had not said much about this link, the audience was feeling the profound love that came with this connection too.

"Glenn was my son," she explained quietly in her own time. You could almost see her thoughts going back to the time when he was alive. I knew that the accident had happened at work and that it had been gruesome. I conveyed this. She nodded and for a moment or two I felt her pain, her loss. Sometimes I do wonder just how people do bear all that they have to deal with. I was not shown the specifics of the accident but it felt as though machinery was involved in some way. I suspect that information was not given because neither I nor some of the audience could have handled the full details very well. Saying it happened at work and was gruesome was clearly sufficient. The lady's facial expression said it all.

Internally I could see a young policeman and Glenn shaking his head. It appeared that he was shaking his head about the policeman for some reason. I was puzzled as to why that would be. It was as though he didn't want the policeman to see his body. Was it that he didn't want the police involved or was it that his body was in such a mess he didn't want anyone to see it? I conveyed what I was seeing.

"I know what he means," Mum was keen to explain. "The police were called after the accident and the police officer on duty was a friend of Glenn's. He had to come to the accident site to investigate and to sight the body and Glenn wouldn't have wanted his friend to see him like that. It would've upset him. It really shook his friend up for quite some time." Glenn's images in my head had made sense and again it was something that I could not possibly have known.

More than anything, Glenn wanted his mum to know that he was now alright, especially after the extreme damage his physical body had suffered. There was something else Glenn also needed to communicate to his mum. He indicated that there had been problems between his wife and his mum before he died and that he was aware that things were still not right between them. Mum confirmed that sadly this was the case. "Love is inclusive," he said. "Love should include everyone." He knew Mum knew this but the implication was that his young wife had yet to learn it. Mum nodded. It made perfect sense to her. He didn't go into any further details, he didn't need to. Mum knew he was alright and that was the most important thing. He had done what he needed to do and he stood back and the message ended.

Three generations of loved ones had managed to get through. The first one, the father-in-law, was really there to assist the others to get through – getting my attention and then lending his energy to assist their communications. The second, her husband, came through to say, "I am sorry, I was at fault." The third, and most important, her precious son, to say, "I am alright," and to alert her to the higher lesson in the situation she found herself in with his wife. If you can see the lesson – in this case that love is inclusive – it sometimes makes the behaviour you are experiencing or dealing with easier to bear.

When we can understand what others are 'having to learn' we don't need to take it personally. It is simply something they have to work through. There was a lot of emotion and a lot of healing, for all concerned, in spirit world and here. I was so glad the message took us into an interval as we all needed a break to assimilate what had happened and reflect on the implications for ourselves and our loved ones.

After the Shows

Sometimes, during a show, it becomes apparent that I need to see a person in the audience privately. It can be for different reasons. Sometimes the message would just be too emotional in front of other people; sometimes there is an aspect of the message that requires privacy; and at other times the reason why I am seeing someone after the show proves not to be what I had expected at all.

A gentleman spirit had pointed out his son to me in the middle of a row towards the back of the theatre. Lighting was subdued for the audience's comfort. As I drew close I could see he was in his 40s, well-dressed and accompanied by a lady whom I took to be his wife or partner. My first question was to make sure that I had the right loved one in spirit with the right loved one here. "I have a gentleman standing to your right and he tells me he is your father. Have you lost your father?" "I may have done," came the response. My puzzled look caused the gentleman in the audience to explain further. He held the microphone away from him and quietly indicated that he didn't know who his father was although the family had their suspicions. Because of the very public nature of the shows, my guides usually steer me clear of adoptions or express them in a way that is comfortable for the recipient of the message. Not this time. I sensed it was a situation I really needed to move on from for the gentleman's sake. "I think we will need to deal with this one privately, if that's okay with you. We can have a talk at the end of the show and find out some more information." He quickly nodded in agreement and so I moved on. Such is the nature of mediumship, that I have to be totally present with each link as they come in and so I continued with the show and with other links and let the father in spirit go until I was free at the end of the show.

Even though it was after 10pm before I was able to sit down with the man and his wife, I was glad that they had decided to stay. Perhaps he would get some clarity about who his father was. But instead of getting less puzzling, the message was about to get more so. The 'father' in spirit wasn't telling. Instead, he explained that the only reason the gentleman here didn't know who his father was, was because his mother hadn't wanted this known. His mother was still alive and still kept her secret. The son confirmed this. The father in spirit had respected the mother's wishes while he was

people's faces when you know and they know that their loved ones really do live on is the most incredible feeling you can imagine. There are often tears along the way but deep down you know that the pain will never be quite as hard to bear again. I feel so privileged to be a part of that.

Sometimes people seek me out to clarify parts of a message received during the show as was the case in the next story. At the end of the show a young teenage girl came to see me with her mother. She was obviously quite desperate and was struggling to hold back the tears. In the second half of the show I do an exercise with the audience where I get them to think of a loved one who has passed over and then ask for a song from them. She explained that she missed her maternal grandmother terribly and she had asked her for a song. The song Granny had given her was *I'm Walking Away*. This title had upset her because she felt that the message Granny was giving her was that she was going away. She didn't want Granny to go and it had made her cry.

I linked with the young girl and found her surrounded by pets. I told her what I was seeing.

"We've recently made a lifestyle choice and we are now running a pet shop," Mum laughed.

I tuned in again and this time found Granny. No, she wasn't saying she was walking away, she explained.

Then she shouted in my ear, "The next line of the song – look at the next one of the song."

It wasn't a song I was that familiar with although I had heard it before. Between the three of us we managed to piece it together: "I'm walking away from the troubles in my life to find a better life. I'm walking away, oh to find a better day."

Granny was actually letting her granddaughter know she was now free from the things that used to trouble her here. She was letting her know she was free of worries and at peace. From originally thinking the message was a negative it transpired that it was actually a positive one. This quick meeting one to one after the show had clarified something that could have continued to distress the granddaughter.

The circumstances of the next story shocked me at the time but again it turned out to be a situation where I judged what was happening rather than trusted that all was happening for the highest good of all concerned. As events unfolded it became clear that there was a good reason for this strange turn of events.

A small queue of people was waiting to see me after one particular show ended. There were five that I felt I needed to see privately for one reason or another. It was the most I had ever agreed to see at the end of a show. Generally the shows end around 9:30pm and we then grab something to eat and pack everything away.

192

I had food ordered but it would be cold by the time I had finished seeing these people. I sent Andrew to get his; at least he might as well have a good dinner. I would be sometime yet.

I arranged to see the people in an annexe that was partitioned off the main room. As I was taking a man and his friend backstage to contact the man's two children in spirit world, one who had died tragically and one who had committed suicide, a lady that none of us knew barged into the private area and demanded to sit in. "I haven't had enough proof," was her explanation for this intrusion. I was completely taken aback. I had never experienced anything like this happening before. "How dare she intrude uninvited into this man's grief," I thought. Fortunately, the man was very obliging and agreed that she could stay. Because of his understanding I didn't feel I could object as much as I wanted too. The incident had upset me so I had to calm myself down, let my feelings towards this woman go, and relax, ready to listen. I had help in letting go, from my spirit guides. A warm flood of unconditional love flowed through my body and I was able to contact both the man's son and daughter in spirit world.

The communication with them was a bit jumbled. It seemed as though the brother and sister were very much together in the spiritual side of life and were communicating with me together. Although it was quite hard to separate their responses initially, by the end of the session the man was happy that it was indeed his two children. The lady who had 'sat in' was also impressed.

When the man and his friend left she asked me to see who was with her. I agreed to do it very quickly, but inside I was feeling quite resentful. I knew there were others waiting, including an elderly couple. What made this lady think her need was greater than the needs of these other people? And what gave her the right to push in? "The quicker I get this over with, the better," I thought. I tuned in and I was so glad I did. The lady's only son in spirit world was with her. He had taken his own life at a young age. *Now* I understood her behaviour. She wasn't really being rude at all – she was just desperate. She blamed herself for her son's death and her grief was all consuming. She was so locked up in her own pain that she hadn't given a thought to how she came across to others. Once I understood how she was suffering, I was sorry I had not been more compassionate towards her before – I had judged her behaviour. She knew her son had problems and had made some very poor choices but she hadn't been able to help him. He came through to tell her that there was nothing that she could have done to stop him and that he was much happier where he now was. It was what she most needed to hear.

The message had been important for the lady and I had been taught an important lesson about not judging a person or a situation. I had not lived that lady's life nor had her experiences. I was in no place to judge her behaviour. I sincerely hoped I would not fall into the same trap again.

The people I see after the shows are also usually the most difficult for me to bear emotionally. Deborah came to see me after a show and asked if I could spare her a few moments. The desperation in her voice was almost tangible – I could see she was not going to accept no for an answer even if it had occurred to me to say so.

"I will do my best," I said. The main part of the theatre was quite dimly lit and so I took her up onto the stage and used the chairs that we had on stage for the show. It was deathly quiet. I did not have to wait long until I saw that a small boy was with her.

"There is a small boy with you – very young – he calls you Mummy. He gives me the name Adam."

"Yes, he was my son," she quickly confirmed as the tears started to flow.

I was shown she had had another son since who was still alive.

"Adam tells me he has a brother who is still here – a brother who would be younger than him."

She nodded in agreement.

As a whole concept Adam showed me that his

mum's concern was that she would also lose his brother. I could feel the anxiety, the fear of loving and losing again. It was almost too much to bear. When she was ready the lady explained that what Adam said made sense. She was concerned that the genetic condition that had taken her first son would also claim her second.

I was shown that her second son had the same condition but was not as badly affected by it. I felt very strongly that her second son would make it and she was very reassured by this. Tests had in fact shown that he did have the same condition but so far his symptoms had not been as bad as those of her first son. She was reassured by my insight as it matched what the doctors and conventional medicine were telling her. I was so glad that I had not seen the second son passing at some stage. What would I have said? She had wanted some reassurance after what she had gone through with her first son. She didn't want to go through it again and I didn't blame her.

Sometimes the stories I see and hear are more than I feel I could bear and I cannot help but feel the deepest respect and compassion for the people who have borne them. There are some amazing people here who have borne incredible adversity and pain and come through it. My life, by comparison, has been easy. We are never given more than we can cope with and I can only conclude that I have come across some very old souls, capable of great love and understanding. If what I do gives any comfort, however small, I am happy to play my part.

Suicide

It was towards the end of a show when I was doing the psychometry demonstration that a young girl in the back row passed me a watch. Immediately I knew the watch wasn't hers; it was her mum's. Then I found myself 'staring' at a lady roughly my own age sitting two rows in front of the girl. At such times, I'm not really staring but I know that is how it often comes across when I'm looking at and beyond someone psychically.

"This is *your* watch," I said, after a pause, pointing at the woman with my finger. The logical part of me was stressing big time. How could I be so bold? My intuitive side knew absolutely that this was so and that the lady was the young girl's mum. How did I know this? Because I had her son, the younger girl's brother with me and he knew them both.

I started to explain what I was experiencing. "I have a young man with me of about 20. He feels like your son and your brother," I said, nodding to the woman and the girl respectively. I knew I was right and their acceptance of this was a mere formality.

He was with me very strongly and he was very distraught. He was very, very emotional and yet he was determined to get through.

"He is very, very sorry – but saying sorry isn't going to make it right – he knows that." After this came out of my mouth I looked across to Mum. She didn't react.

"He is telling me that he took his own life." The audience was hanging on every word. His mum was obviously moved but nonetheless was holding out very well.

Through me he explained, "It was the drugs. I blame the drugs. The drugs affected my thinking and caused my mood swings. I know I had problems before turning to drugs but these were minor compared to the effect the drugs had on me. The drugs made me not 'know' my own mind." The words tumbled out of me and I felt like the son needed to get it all out – to confess all so he also could begin to find peace. Finally there was something important that he wanted his mum to know. "You *were* a good mum. Don't blame yourself for what happened – I know you tried to get through to me."

Mum wasn't able to say much throughout the message because she was very upset. She managed to nod to confirm what I was saying.

After a moment she was able to say, "He's right. I wasn't able to get through to him because of the drugs. He changed so much."

What that woman had been through with her son when he was here and then when he took his own life would have been unbearable for most of us. She was a very advanced soul with a great capacity to love – that doesn't make the pain any less though. In fact I consider such souls feel the pain more. It was confirmed to me that she had been a really good mum to her kids. She hadn't deserved to have this happen, so why had it happened? I honestly didn't know and I didn't know what to say to her other than to reassure her that her son was now alright. Her son couldn't explain why he had done what he did, just that it was the only way he could see at that time. I realised that he had not been passed over long enough to really understand the bigger picture. Perhaps in time he would be able to come through and explain more. Then there could be closure and peace on both sides.

I was glad that he had come through towards the end of the show as the link with him and his family was very emotional and had drained me. As we travelled home from the show, I reflected on how the show had gone. It had gone well in terms of providing evidence but I was disturbed by the level of pain I saw people carrying and having to bear. Like the links I have with children, the links with those who have committed suicide, especially young people, raised questions within me – why? I began asking lots of internal questions about suicide. Why was I coming across so many young people and particularly young men at the shows who had taken their own lives? It seemed that this problem was far more prevalent in New Zealand than in the UK. Why was that I wondered?

Nearly always drugs in some shape or form were involved but why did young people resort to drugs in the first place? Occasionally there had been sexual abuse at a young age but not always by any means. I remembered in the UK coming across groups of young people who were friends and had taken their own lives after they had been using with a Ouija board, but in New Zealand Ouija boards seemed unlikely and they hadn't been referred to in messages I had received. I decided I would be open to being taught about what was going on. I must have still been wondering about suicides as I drifted off to sleep.

The next morning I awoke with an insight. At the point of choosing to take their lives the young men concerned had made the best possible choice out of the options they saw as being available to them. To them it was not a *bad* choice, it was the *only* choice. Sometimes, and I would say in my experience, somewhere between 50% and 75% of the time, the choice was affected by a side-effect of drug use – depression.

I knew from previous insights that one characteristic of depression is low or depressed energy. When you are in a low energy state you can't see 'the wood for the trees'; you can't rise above your present situation and see it for what it is, a situation, *not* your life. Your life is much more than your life situation. Your life has an intrinsic quality that will be there whatever life situation arises. So in the case of young people who reached this critical point they temporarily confused *their life* with *their life situation*. They thought that their life situation was *unchangeable*. I knew what I had been told was significant but I also knew that I didn't have all the pieces of the jigsaw. More would be revealed to me later.

Another show, and this time a connection was made with an older person who had been depressed and committed suicide. Unfortunately, the effect of his depressive state on his wife had not gone after he had passed – he was still around and his depressed feelings hung around with him. He came through for a lady in the audience. His presence was really powerful. He was determined to be the first message in the show.

"Do you know the name Gordon?" I asked the lady I had been pulled towards.

"Yes, that's my husband's name," she said. I could see from her body language that she wouldn't be able to come on stage with me and so I let her remain where she was for the rest of the message.

Gordon showed me that he had been depressed for some time and had ended up by taking his own life. He was around his wife a lot and his doing so was making her feel depressed. "What a message to start a show," I thought. "He is showing me that he took his own life," I said moving closer. I knew that the circumstances around the suicide and the discovery were unpleasant. He had hung himself and she did not find him until some days later. However, I did not reveal this to the lady or the audience – it would have been too much for them to bear. The fact that I knew he had taken his own life was enough for her. She knew beyond doubt it was him. Given the nature of the message and the fact that he was still around and making her depressed also meant that I had to handle this one differently. I suggested that I see her privately after the show.

When loved ones take their own lives there is a very real danger that instead of moving through to the light – connecting more deeply with their own soul/higher aspect – they try to stay around their loved ones on earth. They want us to know they are sorry but their presence with us can confuse us. We feel their despair and depression and combined with our own grief it becomes a lethal combination. In these cases the loved ones have to be helped through to the appropriate place for them spirit world side, which then allows the person here to start to heal and move on with their life.

I suspected I was dealing with a similar situation here as I had previously worked with a lady in the UK. A lady had come to see me for a healing as she had been diagnosed as suffering from a bi-polar condition. I found her deceased husband Robert in her space. He had also hung himself and was full of remorse and anguish. I asked her about her husband's mental state and yes, he had been depressed for a long time.

"Did you suffer from bi-polar before your husband died?" I asked.

"No, not at all," came the response.

I was pretty sure that a lot of the negative emotion in her energetic space was not hers. In the counselling she had been having she hadn't been able to deal with it or process it because it wasn't *her* emotion, it was her late husband's. I talked silently in my head to her husband and explained to him that he was causing a lot of harm to his wife. He said he was afraid of passing over in case he was punished for what he had done or he went to hell. I explained that in lots of ways he was already in 'hell' because of his tormented feelings. I reassured him that spirit world side there would be no judgement of him or punishment. Quite the contrary, on spirit world side they would already know what he had been through, they would know that he had done his best, which is all that any of us can do. When he was ready I helped him to pass through to the appropriate dimension and out of his wife's space. With the negative energy gone the lady immediately felt her spirits lift. She was feeling so much better that she was able to return to work within days, with no recurring 'bi-polar' experiences.

I was glad that the lady from the show with the similar problem took up my offer and came to see me in private.

"Have you had bereavement counselling?" I asked.

"Yes, for the last six months but it isn't really helping," she replied. The parallels between these two cases were becoming interesting.

I connected with her husband and as gently as I could I shared the concerns her late husband had about her. "Have you had thoughts of taking *your* life?" She admitted she had.

I told her about the lady in the UK and explained that I was sure that her husband was having a similar effect on her. I sought her permission to help her husband move through to the appropriate dimension so that he would still be able to visit her but his negative feelings would not affect her so strongly.

"I feel as though there is nowhere left to turn. I need to do something. Yes, please try," came her plea.

Andrew and I worked with her husband and by the next day both of them were more settled and moving on with their individual journeys.

My own thoughts about suicide and what happens to people who take their own lives have developed over the years and I share with you now what I have learned through my own personal experience rather than what I have read in books.

People who commit suicide are not 'sinners' and do not go somewhere else to you and I. In my experience from knowing people here who have committed or attempted suicide, they have been without exception sensitive souls. They have all been people who found this life too harsh, too hard in some way. I have also conversed with a great many people on the spiritual side of life who have committed suicide and in the main this description of sensitive would fit them too.

I have received many teachings about there being no 'right' or 'wrong'. *I* am best placed to make *my* decisions because I have lived *my* life. *You* are best placed to make *your* decisions because you have lived *your* life. It therefore makes sense that we should not judge one another; we cannot judge them or anyone else because we have not lived *their* life. It is very often hard for us to understand why someone we know and love would choose to take their own life. But repeatedly I have seen that at the time they made that choice, it was the best or only choice that they could see. There is no punishment for taking their own life but often they regret it because when they leave their physical body here, the way they were feeling does not miraculously get better, as they thought. In fact, they can initially feel worse because they still feel the same but now they do not have a body. Fortunately they are well supported on the spiritual side of life to come to terms with their decision and to find some kind of peace so that they can at last move on.

This last story is again about a young male who took his own life and gives you an overview of the stages the spirits of people who commit suicide can go through after leaving their physical body.

Gregg had 'gone missing' and his sister contacted me to see if I could help 'track him down'. I tracked him down in spirit word. I had a strong link with him but all I could feel was emotion, distress and terror. It was an unpleasant connection for me to make. The family wanted to know what had happened to him but I was finding it very hard to receive any words. All I kept getting was heightened emotions that completely drained me. I decided to let a couple of days pass to give his spirit time to settle but Gregg had other ideas. He was around me and my family almost constantly but I still couldn't get a message from him. I kept asking him, "What happened? Where is your body?" In return, he just kept giving me his feelings and emotions. It was frustrating and the emotions he was giving me were getting increasingly unbearable. Something clearly had to be done.

It was clear from the level of negative emotion that he had not made the correct transition into the higher spiritual dimensions and was instead on the astrals (one of the lower levels referred to in Chapter 7). I was emotionally run down by this time and so Andrew, my partner, helped him to pass through properly into the higher realms. Within 48 hours he was back – in my dreams and when I was awake – and this time he was communicating with me properly. At last I was able to let his family know what had happened, but it was not an easy thing to do as they still held out hope that he was alive.

Gregg had been so distressed about what he had done, that he wanted desperately to stay here to let his parents know where his body was. However, in staying here he was also holding on tightly to his way of seeing the world and all the emotions he had when he was here, which was why communication had been very difficult and why I was getting all the emotion. It had taken a lot of persuading for Andrew to get him to move on to the higher dimensions and I suspect this was because he was worried that he might not be able to get back to see and talk to his family. When he eventually moved over he could see things for how they truly were and was at last more peaceful. Now he was ready and had come back through me to let Mum and Dad know what had happened. The family was devastated by the communication I was now able to give them but relieved that they at least had some closure.

Gregg explained that he had made the best choice or rather the only choice that he could see at the time and had taken his own life. He assured them that it had not been premeditated. He had been feeling down for some time and recent bad news had just tipped him over the edge. He recognised now that if he had listened more to his feelings rather than suppressing them he would not have tipped like he did.

"It wasn't anyone's fault – I know I kept to myself – don't think you should have seen the warning signs, there weren't any," he continued. Regrets? Yes, he regretted not seeing things differently and he regretted all the pain he had caused everyone but he didn't regret being on the spirit side of life. Now at last he was really starting to understand himself and make sense of things and was moving forward – free of the painful way he used to see things. His journey had begun – it would take time for him to find complete peace.

It is reassuring that in 10 years of working as a medium I have not experienced a dimension that you would call 'hell' nor have I had a spirit describe a place that would match our earthly perception of hell, other than a spirit who, somewhat tongue in cheek, described his life on this earth plane as 'a living hell'. Perhaps this perception is closer to the truth.

It seems that if we do something here that does not rest well with us, we feel it inside. If we continue to do nothing about the situation, we either continue to feel bad or we ignore our feelings, blocking our energy. Neither reaction is satisfactory, and the latter manifests itself as illness or depression. So if we don't make the 'right' choices as guided by our internal feelings we *can* create 'hell' for ourselves while we are here. Whilst there is no 'hell' and no punishment for committing suicide, it is clear that if we had a different perspective on life, suicide is perhaps a choice that we would not make. Let us hope that in the years ahead as humanity becomes more self aware and more conscious we will all listen more intently to those inner feelings that tell us when something is right or not right for us. Let us hope that the suicides of the past will inspire us each to really listen to our inner-most feelings and be true to ourselves every moment of each day, rather than letting things bottle up inside. Let us hope that in being our *true* selves and accepting ourselves *as we are*, we inspire others to do the same. Perhaps then we will create 'heaven' for ourselves here on earth rather than 'hell' and the pain of the suicides that have gone before will not have been in vain.

You Can Do It Too!

I am often asked during question time at my shows 'can anyone do what you do?'. I believe that if you would *love* to do what I do then, yes, you should be able to do it. The spiritual dimensions are much closer than most people realise. I often explore with the audiences at my shows just how psychic they actually are.

I start by asking them some basic questions: "How many of you know who is on the phone when the phone rings?" "How many of you have thought of a person and then unexpectedly bumped into them within hours or days?"

If they can answer yes to either of these questions then they too have some psychic ability. If you also were able to answer yes to either of these questions you also have some psychic ability. What you need to know is how to access this ability and in what ways you can use it. This *is* something you can learn. The more you ask of your intuition (in-tuition or inner teaching) the more it will assist you.

After these simple questions, I do some other basic exercises at the shows to illustrate to people the ways they can begin to explore their own psychic abilities if that is what they wish to do. In this chapter I will share these exercises with you, so you can try them if you wish to.

Connecting with a loved one in spirit world

"Would you like to see if you have someone with you from spirit world?" I asked one audience. Just about every hand in the room went up and so I talked them through the following exercise. It is one you can try yourself at any time as long as you are not down or depressed. Talking to spirits when you are down can cause you to attract ones that are also down, which is not generally a good idea. Alcohol and drugs also need to be avoided before doing exercises such as this or you could attract to yourself earth-bound spirits that just want to enjoy the physical effect of those substances on your body. So you could say that this exercise is best done when you are in 'good spirits' – a common phrase and again much closer to the truth than most people recognise! If you are at all apprehensive about doing these exercises you may want to ask for protection from God, or Christ or your Higher Consciousness, or you may wish to imagine surrounding yourself with light before starting. Protection is not necessary unless *you* feel it is, so if you feel apprehensive in any way, ask for it.

"Okay, start by closing your eyes – by feeling yourself in your body.

Feel your fingers and your toes and the feeling of the chair beneath you.

Give yourself a moment or two to really bring yourself into the present and into your body.

Now feel the real 'you', the energy or essence within your physical body. The part of you that listens to the part of me.

Now think loving thoughts about your loved ones who have passed over."

Usually when I do this with an audience the feeling of the room starts to lift and the place physically starts to feel warmer.

"When you are filled with feelings of love you can intend that a loved one be with you.

You can choose a specific person or put the intent out to the whole of your spirit family."

Take a moment to make your request.

At a show I then ask the following question, three times. I ask the audience to notice the response they get and to notice what happens to their eyelids in particular. Often I find that those who initially have held back now decide to participate in the exercise. As I am not able to ask these questions for you, you will need to ask these questions yourself, internally in your head or get someone else to ask these questions for you.

"Are there any energies or entities with you/me?"
Pause.
"Are there any energies or entities with you/me?"
Pause.
"Are there any energies or entities with you/me?"
Pause for a few moments, keeping your eyes closed. Then open your eyes.

In an audience a lot of talking erupts after this, which usually means people have experienced something. I usually let them talk a while before asking what they have experienced. The discussion would go something like this:

"Okay, how many of you felt your eyelids flickering while we did that?"

About a third of any audience usually raise their hands.

"That means you have the ability to sense spirit – clairsentience," I explain.

So, how did you go? What did you feel? There is no right or wrong signal – just notice what you get. You may find different guides give you different signals. I only mention the flickering eyelids initially because that is the most common phenomenon I personally have witnessed. If you get a different sensation it is no less meaningful, in fact, it probably has more meaning because it is not something I have suggested to you.

Some other ways guides commonly make themselves felt other than by flickering your eyelids are: a cobweb feeling on the face, an itchy nose, tingling or warm ears, tingling in your head, a headache or tingling down the left-hand side of your body, particularly your hand and arm.

Receiving a message

The next exercise is to see if you can receive a message. This time the exercise will check for clairvoyant (clear seeing) and clairaudient (clear hearing) abilities, not just the clairsentient ability.

The exercise starts in exactly the same way as the first exercise. Feeling yourself in your body, thinking loving thoughts about loved ones who have passed over and then intending that a loved one be with you.

After doing this the instructions change. I usually give these instructions at a show, so if you are doing this at home you will need to give the instructions to yourself internally or get someone else to read the instructions to you.

"Ask to be shown who is with you."

Short pause.

"Ask to be given a colour and accept the very first colour you see, sense or hear."

Pause.

"Ask for the name of a song or a line from a song that is significant for you at this stage in your journey."

Open your eyes.

We all have a preferred way of receiving information. This exercise helps to identify it. The colours that people receive each have a meaning. If you are going to do this exercise yourself it is best to read these *after* you do the exercise. If you don't get anything initially do not be disheartened, try again another time and do not try too hard. This should be easy and natural for us – we can all do it.

So what do the colours mean? This is a simple system I have developed to help our guides give a basic message.

Red

You have a lot of energy, which can be a very positive thing but you need more focus or direction. There is a need for knowing your life purpose, simplifying your life and deciding what is important to you.

Orange

Orange indicates that you are very empathetic; able to sense how others are feeling. This can be a great strength, helping you feel compassion for others. In excess, though, our strengths become our weaknesses. Check if the feelings that are running through you are your own or someone else's.

If you are reaching for comfort foods it is time to recognise this – deal with the emotions that are yours and let the others go.

Yellow

Yellow indicates a sharp analytical mind. It can also indicate that you are in your mind too much. Observe yourself and your thoughts. Are you in your mind thinking about the future or the past, rather than being in life? Are you worrying rather than trusting? Know that you are safe. You are part of an incredible creation that we call life. All is as it should be and you have within you all you need. Take time to be here and now and to connect with the earth.

Green

This can indicate one of two things. If you are feeling under the weather it may be a sign that you need to be healed yourself or your guides may be letting you know that you have natural healing abilities and it is time for you to develop them. If you have also had times when your hands went very hot or very cold for no apparent reason the latter is almost certain to apply. I have found that Reiki and Spiritual Healing workshops allow natural abilities to develop in a safe and holistic way. You can find more details on my website, www.jeanettewilson.com.

Blue

Your guide wants to talk with you and wants you to learn how to listen better – it is time to learn to meditate, to still your mind so you can hear what your guides are saying. It is time to pay more attention within.

Purple/Indigo

Your guide is working with you to develop your intuition and psychic abilities especially your third eye in the middle of your eyebrows. Allow your intuition to guide you by asking yourself before you answer the phone: "Who is it on the phone?" "What letters will be in the letterbox?" "Where will I find a car parking space today?" The more we use our intuition the more it will be there for us when we need it. If we don't use it, we lose it.

White/Violet/Gold

You have a higher level guide with you – a master or a teacher of some kind. You can sit and ask them questions about a subject and they will respond – this is sometimes called channelling, which I will explore more in my next book.

Black

Your guides want you to access your unconscious mind more and this can most easily be done through your dreams. It is a good idea to start keeping a dream journal. As you go to sleep ask your guides for a dream to help explain something to you. When you awake lie perfectly still and remember as much as you can of the dream. Do not move during this time or you will lose whole chunks of the dream. When you have replayed the whole of the dream in your head in as much detail as you can, then you can write it down. It is a good idea to write your dreams down as they often make a lot more sense when we look back on them sometime later. To interpret the dream, overlay what happened in the dream and your feelings about it onto your present life situation. Again, there will be more about dreams in my next book.

Pink

Your guides are letting you know that they love you unconditionally. Perhaps this is a time to be more accepting of yourself and your feelings. Perhaps they are just reminding you how much you are loved.

At most shows about 75% of the audience succeeds in getting a colour – if at first you don't succeed try again. If you get a song, the song may be significant for the particular loved one who is with you or it may be significant in terms of what is happening in your life. Spirits often find it easier to communicate with songs rather than words. At one show a lady and her father came through from spirit world before the show had even started. I could hear her singing *Danny Boy* as I changed in the dressing room. As I went on stage she pointed out her husband to me. She had passed before her father and her husband had fond memories of watching her singing *Danny Boy* to her father, whose name was Danny, before she died. The song was her way of showing that it was her and also that her father Danny who had passed more recently

219

was with her and they were together once more in spirit world.

Another time the song I was given related to the phase someone was going through in their life. I received the song, *I Promised You a Miracle* and it transpired that the young couple were trying for a baby. Spirit world was just letting them know that their fondest wish was about to be fulfilled.

In the same way, you can receive songs when you do the previous exercise. The meaning of the song should make sense to you in some way. If it doesn't ask to be shown why that particular song is significant to you and then be completely open to the response you get, it may not be the one you expect.

Once you have had your first communication with a loved one you may also be interested in meeting one of your guides. We all have guides that are there to help us who may or may not be family members. This exercise helps you to sense or meet them for the first time.

Meeting your guide

"Start by closing your eyes. Feel yourself in your body – feel yourself here and now in this body.

Feel your breathing – notice it but do not try to change it.

Feel your fingers and your toes and the feeling of the chair beneath you."

Now it is time to intend that one of your guides be present with you. You may or may not sense them come close. Either way, go on to the next part of the exercise.

Say (in your head):

"When you mean yes do this to me," and rock yourself backwards and forwards for a few moments from your waist and hips.

If you feel awkward doing this, you are not alone. Audiences often look at me as if to say, "You're not serious are you?" I look back and say, "I sure am!" Persevere because the experience is worth it. Trust me, I used to be a bank manager.

Make sure the rocking sensation is really strong and remember that at this stage you are moving *yourself*.

Then say to yourself, *"And when you mean no do this to me,"* and move from left to right.

Then stand perfectly still with your eyes closed and say, *"Is there anyone with me?"*

Be *open* to what happens.

When they ask this final question most people find themselves physically pushed forwards or backwards. If you don't, try it again. Be sure to relax.

When our guides or loved ones come in close, it is not only possible for us to sense them physically; they can also do things like ring door bells or phones, flicker lights or move keys to stop or delay us going somewhere. Our guides or loved ones simply lower their vibration so they can be felt here and use their will power to affect us.

If you want to take this exercise one stage further, repeat the exercise but this time ask the guide the following questions.

"Are you male or female?"

Be open to seeing them, sensing them or hearing them.

"Are you young or old?"

"What is your name?"

"Can you show me what you look like?"

Ask the questions in such a way that you leave a pause after each to see which sense is the easiest or most natural for you to use – clairsentience (feeling), clairaudience (hearing) or clairvoyance (seeing). I have found that the most common ability tends to be a feeling but there are always a surprising number of people at the shows who also hear a name or glimpse their loved one in spirit world.

At the end of the exercise, thank your guide and other helpers for their assistance.

I would say about 30% of the people in the audiences are able to discern who it is that is with them at their very first attempt – a result most are thrilled with. Communication with the spiritual realms is getting easier and easier all the time, but we don't know how easy it is unless we give it a try. Your guides are always with you *wanting* to help but the door opens from *this* side. If *you* don't ask, *you* don't get.

Guides often present themselves as wise men or women or religious figures such as nuns or monks, native American Indians, ancient Chinese elders and so on. I feel this may be just our brain putting a familiar image to the wisdom we perceive and our guides may or may not be as we see them. It took several years for my guides to give me their names and I think this is because names limit them in some way. Don't get too worried if you can't see your guides. I have only ever seen mine once, however, I often sense their presence strongly and experience them as feelings, sensations and as white/golden light.

Increasingly at the shows I have come across significant numbers of people who want to be able to do what I can do, so I have started putting my thoughts into a book of straightforward methods to develop intuition and psychic abilities. This will be in my next book *Dare to Believe*.

One of the reasons for learning to do what I do to the level I do it, is to be able to share this knowledge with others. I want others to be able to do it without needing to belong to any particular religious group. The more people who are able to see loved ones in spirit world, the better, as that then helps everyone else to see them as well. This works in more than one way.

Firstly, as more people learn how to see and communicate with spirit world, increasingly this knowledge will be accepted and can expand and spread. Secondly, the '100th monkey effect' will take effect. Let me explain the background to this.

A female monkey on an island was observed washing her sweet potatoes in a stream before eating them. Before very long all the monkeys of her group also started washing their sweet potatoes. What surprised the scientists studying the monkeys was that *at that same time* monkeys on a neighbouring island *also* started washing their potatoes. This had not been observed happening before this point. The two islands were sufficiently far away that it was impossible that the monkeys could have travelled from one island to another. How did this transfer of knowledge happen? The scientists concluded that the monkeys shared a 'consciousness' at some level. Once sufficient monkeys on the first island were washing their sweet potatoes, this knowledge was somehow transferred to the group of monkeys on the other island. This is known as the '100th monkey effect'.

In the same way, if a certain number of people can see and converse with spirit world, this shared consciousness will sooner or later transfer to others to the point where we will *all* be able to do it. I hope it will be in my lifetime.

Imagine how life would be if we could all tap into our psychic abilities.

We would know when natural disasters were about to hit just like the animals do and get our families and ourselves into safe places.

Lying by individuals, companies or governments would become a thing of the past because we would all see through it.

We would all know instinctively what was right for us and make better choices for our families and ourselves.

We would be able to talk to loved ones and guides at will and be able to understand more about ourselves and this incredible journey we call life.

We would know absolutely that there was nothing to fear and that in turn would give us peace, allowing us to love and be loved more than ever before.

No wonder our loved ones in spirit world are so keen to help us know they are there. By awaking us to their existence they start to open our hearts and minds to the true nature of reality. They start replacing the fear that we have held, often unconsciously, with *love*. They start us thinking about what is possible and remind us of who we truly are – eternal beings partaking in an incredible journey.

We would at last find peace and that in itself has huge implications for mankind.

Epilogue

Having had the experiences I have had I now know that nothing ever happens by chance – all is interconnected. People do not come to my shows by chance; their loved ones in spirit bring them. They may attract the person's attention to an advertisement for the show or they may work through a family member or friend to get them there. In the same way people have also told me that they were drawn to my first book *Medium Rare*. Have you ever wondered how you came to be reading this book? I can assure you it is not by chance! There were a number of things that happened in 2004 that seem to suggest that the universe conspired to ensure my books got published and this gave me confidence that what I had to say would help people. As an addition to my show stories, I'd like to share this very special story with you.

It was becoming increasingly clear that the people I was seeing at the shows needed more than I could give them in a two-hour show. The same questions were coming up over and over again, and the time they took to answer was eating into the mediumship time. I recognised that there was a wealth of information that I could share and as I received more and more requests for a book about my experiences so it became clear that this would be the next logical step for me. Over a couple of months I pulled a book together with the idea of self-publishing it and giving it out at shows. I got a quotation from an out-of-town printer while we were touring and then decided to get a second one from a local company.

I liaised with someone from Zenith Print and Design with regard to the book cover and binding options. I looked at paper samples and awaited the print quote. Before it arrived, I received a call from the marketing manager of Zenith Publishing. She wanted to know if I was firm in my resolve to self-publish or would I consider being published?

Was I hearing correctly? I thought the company I had visited the day before was just a printer. I didn't know there was also a publishing arm. We arranged a meeting for later that day. Andrew and I were surprised – I had known people who had written books and not been able to get them published anywhere, so I hadn't even investigated that route myself.

It transpired that Zenith Publishing was a new general publishing arm of the company. After many years of being primarily an educational publisher they were broadening out. One of the genres they were looking to publish in was mind, body, spirit. They had identified this as an area of increasing interest in the market-place and saw the growing potential in it. I left my book with them to read and assess. I wasn't confident of a positive outcome, as they seemed too mainstream to take on someone like me. They printed schoolbooks and I talked to the dead!

However, at a subsequent meeting they explained they could see the potential in my book (they liked the idea of bank manager to medium) and were interested in talking further. The problem was that the book I had written was really several books. I had tried to answer everyone's questions in the one book, so there was something on everything. We discussed what books we should begin with and it was decided that the first book should be my life story and go from there. We negotiated a contract and the writing began. What an exciting turn of events. My first book, *Medium Rare*, was released in July 2004 and made the bestseller list, and now this, my second book, is also written and published for your enjoyment and enlightenment.

A simple story I hear you say. Where does the universe come in? Where's the interconnectedness of all things? I had already recognised that here were several 'coincidences'. Zenith had just moved to general publishing and had chosen the mind, body, spirit genre – quite a change. "OK," I hear you say, "there are certainly a few things falling into place but not *that* convincing." But there's more. After the book had been published I found out about some of the things that happened *behind* the scenes that along with these things confirmed my initial reflections – the universe was indeed at work.

Raewynne, the marketing manager, had moved to Taranaki from Auckland. After a break from publishing for a year she was delighted to see an ad in the paper for a marketing manager at Zenith Publishing. She didn't even know there was a publisher in town. It was her suggestion that the company include mind, body, spirit in their general publishing stable and she had suggested a series of books would be a good thing to look out for.

Alessandra, who had been employed in the marketing department at Zenith Publishing for only three weeks, was involved in the meetings with me along with the directors and the marketing manager. She recognised me and explained that she had been to one of my recent shows. Her husband had helped organise a Hawera show a few months earlier as part of his work and she had come to assist him with refreshments at half time. So by chance she had seen me in action and was impressed and obviously had been able to inform the others of this. I was pleased she was there as I had a sense that she would be 'on my side' and able to vouch for my ability as a medium first hand.

So the evidence builds. Raewynne found a publisher where she didn't expect to and it was her suggestion that mind, body, spirit be one area of focus for the new general publishing at Zenith. Alessandra was very new in the job and had been to my show. Had I called in earlier, Alessandra would not have been there and no one there would have known my name, or whether I could do what I said I could as a medium.

But how did the publishing staff find out about my request for a printing quotation? The two arms (print and publishing) work separately and it could have been that my print request could have been responded to and nobody else within the organisation would have known and pursued it further. This is the bit where the hairs on my arms go on end.

This is how the connection was made. Walking through the car park one wet afternoon at the end of the business day a piece of paper blew up and onto Alessandra's feet. She picked it up and on it were my name and phone number. She recognised my name from the Hawera show and passed it to Raewynne who was just about to set off in her car. "I know this is important," Alessandra said as she thrust the soggy piece of paper into Raewynne's hand. Thankfully, Raewynne followed up on her colleague's strong inner knowing and the rest you know. If this piece of paper hadn't been in the car park and had not been picked up by the *only* person within the organisation who knew who I was, none of what has developed since would have happened.

The final piece of the jigsaw was the part that made me cry when I heard about it. The day that Alessandra found the piece of paper in the carpark was the anniversary of the day Alessandra's mother had died. Even in death Alessandra's mother was guiding her. I was supposed to write and the universe was confirming that for me by arranging for my books to be published. Alessandra now works as my personal assistant and publicist with her mum's blessing.

So you see there is no way that you are reading this book by chance – you are reading it because you are supposed to. Perhaps it will awaken something in you or remind you of something long forgotten. Perhaps it will help you find peace or move on with your life. Whatever it does for you, I hope it also helps you to remember that there is a whole universe out there waiting to support you on your journey – if you let it.

All you have to do is ask!

If you would like information about Jeanette's shows, workshops or television appearances please visit www.jeanettewilson.com.